T0392268

Arduino Programming using Simulink

Published 2025 by River Publishers

River Publishers

Broagervej 10, 9260 Gistrup, Denmark

www.riverpublishers.com

Distributed exclusively by Routledge

605 Third Avenue, New York, NY 10017, USA

4 Park Square, Milton Park, Abingdon, Oxon OX14 4RN

Arduino Programming using Simulink / by Majid Pakdel.

Routledge is an imprint of the Taylor & Francis Group, an informa business

ISBN 978-87-4380-081-1 (paperback)

ISBN 978-87-4380-083-5 (online)

ISBN 978-87-4380-082-8 (ebook master)

A Publication in the River Publishers Series in Rapids

Arduino Programming using Simulink

Majid Pakdel

MISCO, Mianeh, Iran

NEW YORK AND LONDON

Contents

Preface

Arduino is a popular open-source electronics platform that has revolutionized the world of DIY electronics and prototyping. With its easy-to-use hardware and software, Arduino has enabled countless individuals and companies to create innovative projects and solutions.

Simulink is a powerful tool for modeling, simulating, and analyzing dynamic systems. By combining Simulink with Arduino, we can create complex control systems and algorithms for a wide range of applications.

This book, "Arduino Programming using Simulink," is a comprehensive guide for beginners and experienced users alike to learn how to program Arduino using Simulink. We will explore how to design and implement Static Var Compensator (SVC) systems and Dynamic Voltage Restorer (DVR) systems using Simulink, and then transfer the code to the Arduino IDE for real-time implementation.

Through hands-on examples and practical exercises, readers will gain a solid understanding of the principles behind Arduino programming, Simulink modeling, and control system design. By the end of this book, you will be equipped with the knowledge and skills to create your own advanced projects and contribute to the exciting world of Arduino programming.

All the code from the book can be found on GitHub at the following link: https://github.com/Majid-Pakdel/book-codes.

We hope you find this book to be a valuable resource in your journey of exploring Arduino and Simulink together. Happy programming!

About the Author

Majid Pakdel received his Bachelor's degree in Electrical-Telecommunications Engineering from Amirkabir University of Technology, Tehran in 2004, his Master's degree in Electrical power Engineering from Isfahan University of Technology in 2007, his Ph.D. in Electrical power Engineering from University of Zanjan in 2018, and his Master's degree in Computer Engineering – Artificial Intelligence and Robotics from Malek Ashtar University of Technology, Tehran in 2023. He has published over 20 papers and 7 books in the fields of electrical engineering and computer science. He was a visiting Ph.D. student in the Department of Energy Technology at Aalborg University between 2015 and 2016.

Introduction to Static Var Compensator (SVC)

1.1 Introduction

A power system is a network of electrical components used to supply, transmit, and distribute electricity. It consists of generators, transformers, transmission lines, and distribution networks. The reliability and stability of a power system are crucial for ensuring a constant and efficient supply of electricity to consumers. One of the key challenges in power systems is maintaining the voltage and reactive power levels within acceptable limits.

Voltage is the electrical potential difference between two points in a circuit, expressed in volts. It is essential to ensure that voltage levels are maintained within acceptable limits to prevent damage to electrical equipment and ensure the reliable operation of the power system. Reactive power, on the other hand, is the component of power that oscillates between the source and load due to the inductive and capacitive elements in the electrical network. It plays a crucial role in the operation and control of power systems.

In a power system, reactive power control is necessary to maintain the voltage levels within the desired range. Reactive power control devices, such as capacitors and inductors, are used to manage the flow of reactive power and stabilize the voltage levels. However, conventional methods of reactive power control have limitations in terms of response time and flexibility.

A Static Var Compensator is a voltage-source converter-based device used for voltage and reactive power control in power systems. It consists of semiconductor devices, such as thyristors or insulated gate bipolar transistors

(IGBTs), connected to a transformer to provide fast and precise control of reactive power.

The primary function of an SVC is to regulate voltage and reactive power levels in a power system by providing or absorbing reactive power as needed. It can compensate for fluctuations in load conditions, improve system stability, and enhance power quality. SVCs are typically installed at strategic locations in the power system, such as at the point of common coupling between utility grids or at substations, to support voltage regulation and enhance system performance.

SVCs offer several advantages over conventional reactive power compensation devices, such as faster response times, reduced power losses, and improved system efficiency. They can operate in both capacitive and inductive modes, providing more flexibility in voltage control applications. Additionally, SVCs can be easily integrated into existing power systems without significant modifications, making them a cost-effective solution for improving system reliability and performance.

An SVC is a dynamic device that continuously monitors system conditions and adjusts its reactive power output to maintain voltage stability and improve power quality. The primary components of an SVC include the inverter, transformer, and control system. The inverter consists of semiconductor devices that convert DC power into AC power, allowing the SVC to inject or absorb reactive power as needed. The transformer is used to step up or step down the voltage level to match the system requirements. The control system, on the other hand, monitors system parameters, such as voltage and current levels, and calculates the required reactive power compensation.

There are several control strategies used in SVCs to regulate voltage and reactive power levels in power systems. The most common control strategies include fixed capacitor control, voltage control mode, and reactive power control mode. Fixed capacitor control operates the SVC in a fixed capacitor mode to maintain the system voltage within acceptable limits. Voltage control mode adjusts the output voltage of the SVC to regulate the system voltage level. The reactive power control mode dynamically adjusts the reactive power output of the SVC to stabilize the system voltage and improve the power factor.

SVCs offer several advantages over traditional reactive power compensation devices, such as capacitors and synchronous condensers, in terms of response time, flexibility, and control capability.

One of the key benefits of SVCs is their ability to provide fast and precise control of reactive power, allowing for rapid response to changes in system conditions. This enables SVCs to stabilize system voltage and improve power quality, reducing the likelihood of voltage sags, swells, and fluctuations. SVCs also help to enhance system stability by damping voltage and frequency oscillations, ensuring a reliable and secure power supply to consumers.

Another advantage of SVCs is their flexibility in voltage control applications. SVCs can operate in both capacitive and inductive modes, enabling them to provide reactive power support in a wide range of system conditions. This flexibility allows for optimal utilization of the SVCs in various power system configurations, enhancing system efficiency and performance.

SVCs also offer energy savings and reduced operating costs by improving the power factor and reducing reactive power losses in the system. By providing reactive power support only when needed, SVCs help to minimize power wastage and optimize system operation. This results in lower electricity bills for consumers and improved overall system efficiency.

SVCs are commonly used in transmission and distribution systems to provide voltage and reactive power control at critical locations, such as substations, interconnections, and industrial plants.

One of the primary applications of SVCs is in voltage regulation at the point of common coupling between utility grids. SVCs installed at these locations can help to stabilize system voltage and maintain power quality by providing reactive power support to the grid. This ensures a smooth and reliable transfer of power between different interconnected systems, reducing the risk of voltage instability and equipment damage.

SVCs are also used in distribution systems to improve the voltage profile and power factor at substations and load centers. By installing SVCs at these locations, utilities can reduce line losses, enhance voltage stability, and improve system efficiency. This allows for efficient distribution of electricity to consumers, minimizing downtime, and improving overall system reliability.

In industrial applications, SVCs are used to provide reactive power support to large motor drives, arc furnaces, and other non-linear loads. By compensating for the reactive power demand of these loads, SVCs help to stabilize system voltage and reduce harmonic distortion. This ensures the smooth operation of industrial equipment and prevents damage to power system components, enhancing system reliability and performance.

Designing an SVC involves determining the appropriate rating, configuration, and control strategy based on the system requirements and operating conditions. The installation of an SVC requires careful planning and coordination to ensure proper integration with the existing power system infrastructure.

The first step in designing an SVC is to assess the reactive power requirements of the system and determine the optimal rating of the SVC. The rating of an SVC is determined based on factors such as the maximum reactive power demand, voltage regulation requirements, and system impedance. The reactive power rating of the SVC should be sufficient to compensate for fluctuations in reactive power demand and maintain system voltage within acceptable limits.

The next step in designing an SVC is to select the appropriate configuration based on the system layout and voltage control requirements. SVCs can be installed in various configurations, such as single-line, double-line, or multi-line configurations, depending on the system topology and voltage regulation needs. The configuration of the SVC should be chosen to optimize system performance, minimize losses, and enhance voltage stability.

Once the rating and configuration of the SVC are determined, the next step is to select the control strategy based on the system operating conditions and control objectives. The control strategy of an SVC can be fixed capacitor control, voltage control mode, or reactive power control mode, depending on the desired system response and control requirements. The control system of the SVC should be designed to provide fast and accurate control of reactive power and voltage levels in the system.

The final step in designing an SVC is to evaluate the installation requirements and site conditions to ensure proper integration with the existing power system infrastructure. The installation of an SVC requires coordination with various stakeholders, such as utilities, system operators, and equipment suppliers, to ensure a seamless deployment of the SVC. The physical layout, electrical connections, and communication interface of the SVC should be designed to meet the technical requirements and safety standards of the power system.

The rapid advancement in power electronics technology and control systems has led to the development of new concepts and applications for SVCs, opening up new possibilities for improving system reliability and performance.

One of the key trends in SVC technology is the integration of advanced control algorithms and communication systems to enhance the dynamic response and flexibility of SVCs. Advanced control algorithms, such as model predictive control and adaptive control, are being used to optimize the operation of SVCs in real-time and adapt to changing system conditions. Communication systems, such as SCADA networks and IoT devices, are being used to enable remote monitoring and control of SVCs, allowing operators to manage the device from anywhere in the world.

Another trend in SVC technology is the development of modular and scalable designs that allow for easy deployment and expansion of SVCs in power systems. Modular SVCs consist of multiple units that can be connected in parallel or in series to provide the desired reactive power output. Scalable designs enable operators to increase or decrease the capacity of the SVC to meet changing system requirements and load conditions. This flexibility allows for optimal utilization of SVCs in various power system configurations and ensures cost-effective solutions for voltage control applications.

The integration of energy storage systems with SVCs is another emerging trend in power systems, enabling the storage of excess energy generated by renewable sources and the provision of reactive power support during high demand periods. Energy storage systems, such as batteries and supercapacitors, can be combined with SVCs to enhance system performance, improve voltage stability, and reduce system losses. By storing and releasing energy as needed, energy storage systems help to optimize the operation of SVCs and ensure a reliable and secure power supply to consumers.

Figure 1.1 represents the simplified scheme of a Static Var Compensator (SVC).

Figure 1.1: A simplified scheme of a Static Var compensator.

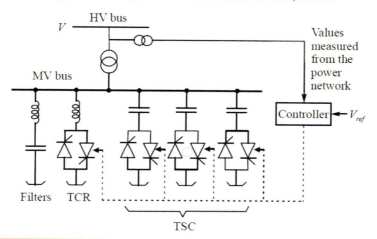

The thyristor-controlled reactor (TCR) is a form of continuously controlled inductance, ranging from no inductance (when thyristors are blocked) to maximum inductance (when thyristors are fully conducting). The thyristor-switched capacitors (TSCs) are controlled using static devices. Through proper control of the TCR, a range of control is achieved for the Static Var Compensator (SVC)

from maximum inductive to maximum capacitive. This setup allows the SVC to generate or absorb the precise amount of reactive power needed, with fixed filters primarily used for low-order harmonics filtering created by the TCR. The capacitors in the filters also contribute to the generation of reactive power. Pairs of anti-parallel connected thyristors ensure conduction on both cycles of the voltage waveform. Both thyristors in the pair must remain in conduction, or a command impulse is required at the start of each cycle controlled by the respective thyristor in order to maintain a constant current through the capacitor and/or reactor. If the command impulse is interrupted, the current through the thyristor will not immediately cease, and it will only be blocked at the natural zero crossing of the voltage. This is the moment when the other thyristor in the valve can be turned on.

1.2 Thyristor-controlled Reactor (TCR)

A typical thyristor-controlled reactor consists of a fixed reactor of inductance L and a bidirectional thyristor valve, as shown in Figure 1.2.

Figure 1.2: A typical thyristor-controlled reactor.

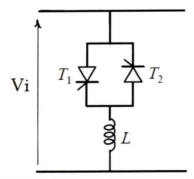

We assume the input voltage to be as in the equation below

$$V_i = V_m \cos(\omega t). \tag{1.1}$$

Also, we assume the thyristor T_1 is fired at an angle of α (rad), therefore, the current flowing through inductor L can be written as

$$i = \frac{V_m}{X_L} \int_\alpha^{\omega t} \cos(\omega t) \, d\omega t, \tag{1.2}$$

where we have

$$X_L = L\omega. \tag{1.3}$$

We can rewrite equation (1.2) as

$$i = \frac{V_m}{X_L} \left[\sin(\omega t) - \sin(\alpha)\right]. \tag{1.4}$$

Now, if T_1 is triggered at $\alpha = 0$ we will have

$$i = \frac{V_m}{X_L} \sin(\omega t). \tag{1.5}$$

Figure 1.3: The voltage and current waveforms in TCR.

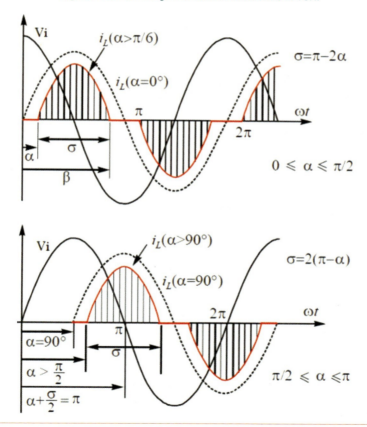

The voltage and current waveforms in TCR are depicted in Figure 1.3. So, when $\alpha = 0$, no current harmonics are generated, and when $\alpha \neq 0$, the current harmonics are generated; since the current waveforms in the positive half cycle and negative half cycle are identical, only the odd harmonics are generated. By using the Fourier series, we have

$$I_1\left(\alpha\right) = \frac{V_m}{X_L}\left[1 - \frac{2\alpha}{\pi} - \frac{\sin\left(2\alpha\right)}{\pi}\right]. \qquad (1.6)$$

If $\alpha = 0$, we can write the equation below

$$I_1 = \frac{V_m}{X_L}. \qquad (1.7)$$

If $\alpha = \pi/2$, we will have the following equation

$$I_1 = 0. \qquad (1.8)$$

We should note that, in this case, the α range is between 0 and $\pi/2$ radians. The plot of I_1 against the firing angle α, is illustrated in Figure 1.4.

Figure 1.4: The plot of I_1 against the firing angle α.

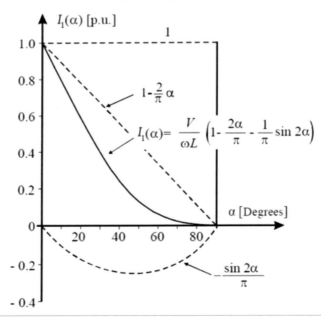

From equation (1.6), we can obtain the following equation

$$\frac{I_1}{V_m} = \frac{1}{X_L}\left[1 - \frac{2\alpha}{\pi} - \frac{\sin\left(2\alpha\right)}{\pi}\right]. \qquad (1.9)$$

We can rewrite equation (1.9) as

$$B_{TCR} = B_L \left[1 - \frac{2\alpha}{\pi} - \frac{\sin(2\alpha)}{\pi} \right], \qquad (1.10)$$

where we have the following equations

$$B_{TCR} = \frac{I_1}{V_m}, \qquad (1.11)$$

$$B_L = \frac{1}{X_L}. \qquad (1.12)$$

The plot of B_{TCR} against the firing angle α is shown in Figure 1.5.

Figure 1.5: The plot of B_{TCR} against the firing angle α.

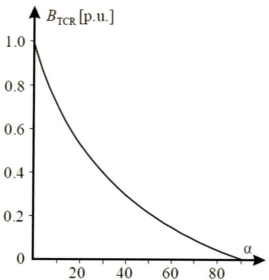

As you can see from Figures 1.4 and 1.5, the admittance $B_{TCR}(\alpha)$ varies in the same manner as the fundamental current $I_1(\alpha)$ against the firing angle α. When $\alpha = 0$, then the TCR becomes a TSR (thyristor switched reactor).

The following procedures are used to get the current equation of the TCR.

Suppose we have the following equation

$$V_s = V_i = V_m \sin(\omega t) . \qquad (1.13)$$

During the thyristor conduction we have

$$V_s = V_L. \tag{1.14}$$

Also, we can write the following equation

$$V_L = L\frac{di}{dt}. \tag{1.15}$$

Therefore, we obtain

$$di = \frac{V_m}{L\omega}\sin(\omega t)d(\omega t). \tag{1.16}$$

By applying integral operation on both sides of equation (1.16), we get

$$\int di = \int_\alpha^{\omega t} \frac{V_m}{L\omega}\sin(\omega t)d(\omega t). \tag{1.17}$$

Therefore, we can write

$$i = \frac{V_m}{L\omega}\left[-\cos(\omega t)\right] + C. \tag{1.18}$$

We know that the following equation is valid

$$i\,|(\omega t = \alpha) = 0, \tag{1.19}$$

therefore, we have

$$C = \frac{V_m}{L\omega}\cos(\alpha). \tag{1.20}$$

By obtaining the value of C, we can write equation (1.18) as

$$i = \frac{V_m}{L\omega}\left[\cos(\alpha) - \cos(\omega t)\right]. \tag{1.21}$$

We know that, in this case, the delay angle α is measured from $\omega t = \pi/2$, therefore we can write

$$\alpha = \alpha' + \pi/2 \text{ and } \omega t = \omega t' + \pi/2. \tag{1.22}$$

If we insert equation (1.22) into equation (1.21), we obtain

$$i = \frac{V_m}{L\omega}\left[\sin(\omega t') - \sin(\alpha')\right]. \tag{1.23}$$

For simplicity and just for a change in notation, we use the following equation

$$\alpha' = \alpha \text{ and } \omega t' = \omega t. \tag{1.24}$$

So, we can write equation (1.23) as

$$i_{TCR} = i\left(\omega t\right) = \frac{V_m}{L\omega}\left[\sin(\omega t) - \sin\left(\alpha\right)\right]. \tag{1.25}$$

For $\alpha = \pi/2$ the $i\left(\omega t\right)$ is continuous; however, for $\alpha > \pi/2$, the $i\left(\omega t\right)$ is discontinuous and rich in harmonics. By using Fourier series, we can write

$$i\left(\omega t\right) = \frac{a_0}{2} + \sum_{n=1}^{\infty} a_n \cos\left(n\omega t\right) + \sum_{n=1}^{\infty} b_n \sin\left(n\omega t\right). \tag{1.26}$$

There is no DC current in the TCR, so we have

$$a_0 = 0. \tag{1.27}$$

Since, $i\left(\omega t\right)$ has odd symmetry, then we can write the following equation

$$a_n = 0. \tag{1.28}$$

Therefore, we get

$$i\left(\omega t\right) = \sum_{n=1}^{\infty} b_n \sin\left(n\omega t\right), \tag{1.29}$$

where b_n is equal to

$$b_n = \frac{2}{\pi} \int_{\alpha}^{\pi-\alpha} i\left(\omega t\right)\sin\left(n\omega t\right)d\left(\omega t\right). \tag{1.30}$$

For $n = 1$ (fundamental component of TCR current) we will have

$$b_1 = \frac{2}{\pi} \int_{\alpha}^{\pi-\alpha} \frac{V_m}{L\omega}\left[\sin(\omega t) - \sin\left(\alpha\right)\right]\sin\left(\omega t\right)d\left(\omega t\right). \tag{1.31}$$

We can rewrite equation (1.31) as follows

$$b_1 = \frac{2V_m}{\pi L\omega} \int_{\alpha}^{\pi-\alpha}\left[\sin^2(\omega t) - \sin\left(\alpha\right)\sin(\omega t)\right]d(\omega t). \tag{1.32}$$

We can obtain the following equation from equation (1.32)

$$b_1 = \frac{2V_m}{\pi L\omega} \int_{\alpha}^{\pi-\alpha}\left[\frac{1-\cos\left(2\omega t\right)}{2} - \sin\left(\alpha\right)\sin\left(\omega t\right)\right]d\left(\omega t\right). \tag{1.33}$$

If we separate the integrals, we can get the equation below.

$$b_1 = \frac{2V_m}{\pi L\omega}\left[\int_{\alpha}^{\pi-\alpha}\frac{1}{2}d\left(\omega t\right) - \frac{1}{2}\int_{\alpha}^{\pi-\alpha}\cos\left(2\omega t\right)d\left(\omega t\right)\right.$$
$$\left. -\sin\left(\alpha\right)\int_{\alpha}^{\pi-\alpha}\sin\left(\omega t\right)d(\omega t)\right]. \tag{1.34}$$

If we solve the integrals of equation (1.34), we can get the following equation

$$b_1 = \frac{2V_m}{\pi L\omega} \left[\frac{1}{2} \left[\pi - \alpha - \alpha \right] - \frac{1}{2} \left[\frac{1}{2} \sin(2\omega t) \right]_{\alpha}^{\pi-\alpha} \right.$$
$$\left. -\sin(\alpha) \left[-\cos(\omega t) \right]_{\alpha}^{\pi-\alpha} \right]. \tag{1.35}$$

For simplification, we can obtain the following equation.

$$b_1 = \frac{2V_m}{\pi L\omega} \left[\frac{1}{2} \left[\pi - 2\alpha \right] - \frac{1}{4} \left[\sin2(\pi-\alpha) - \sin2\alpha \right] \right.$$
$$\left. +\sin(\alpha) \left[\cos(\pi-\alpha) - \cos(\alpha) \right] \right]. \tag{1.36}$$

Therefore, we can rewrite equation (1.36) as

$$b_1 = \frac{2V_m}{\pi L\omega} \left[\frac{1}{2} \left[\pi - 2\alpha \right] - \frac{1}{4} \left[-2\sin(2\alpha) \right] + \sin(\alpha) \left[-2\cos(\alpha) \right] \right]. \tag{1.37}$$

For more simplification, we can obtain the following equation.

$$b_1 = \frac{2V_m}{\pi L\omega} \left[\frac{1}{2}\pi - \alpha + \frac{1}{2}\sin(2\alpha) - \sin(2\alpha) \right]$$
$$= \frac{2V_m}{\pi L\omega} \left[\frac{1}{2}\pi - \alpha - \frac{1}{2}\sin(2\alpha) \right]. \tag{1.38}$$

Finally, we reach

$$b_1 = \frac{V_m}{L\omega} \left[1 - \frac{2\alpha}{\pi} - \frac{1}{\pi}\sin(2\alpha) \right]. \tag{1.39}$$

Therefore, we can write

$$i_1(\omega t) = i_1(\alpha) = b_1 \sin(\omega t). \tag{1.40}$$

So, the peak value of TCR current is as in the equation below

$$I_1(\alpha) = \frac{V_m}{L\omega} \left[1 - \frac{2\alpha}{\pi} - \frac{1}{\pi}\sin(2\alpha) \right]. \tag{1.41}$$

We know that the following equation is valid.

$$I_1(\alpha) = V_m B_{TCR}, \tag{1.42}$$

where, B_{TCR} (TCR susceptance) is equal to

$$B_{TCR} = \frac{1}{L\omega} \left[1 - \frac{2\alpha}{\pi} - \frac{1}{\pi}\sin(2\alpha) \right]. \tag{1.43}$$

We can rewrite equation (1.43) as

$$B_{TCR} = B_{max} \left[1 - \frac{2\alpha}{\pi} - \frac{1}{\pi} \sin\left(2\alpha\right) \right], \qquad (1.44)$$

where, we have

$$B_{max} = \frac{1}{L\omega} \quad @\alpha = 0. \qquad (1.45)$$

So, we can say that when α is increased, the B_{TCR} and also $I_1(\alpha)$ are decreased. In practice, the TCR can operate within a defined $V{-}I$ area which is limited by the maximum admittance, voltage, and current, as depicted in Figure 1.6.

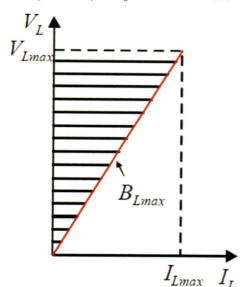

Figure 1.6: Operating $V{-}I$ area of the TCR.

In this book, we will use a three-phase six-pulse TCR in our SVC topology, as shown in Figure 1.7.

We have divided the reactor into two parts so that when an inductor part is short circuited the other part protects the flow of high current through the thyristors, preventing damage to the thyristors. Also, the delta-connected TCR is preferred to star-connected TCR, since it prevents circulation of triplet current harmonics (3, 9, 15, 21, etc.) into the transmission line. In general, $h = 6k + 3$ (where $k = 0, 1, 2, 3\ldots$) harmonic line currents are absent in a three-phase six-pulse delta-connected TCR. Also, in general, $h = 6k \pm 1$ (where $k = 1, 2, 3 \ldots$)

Figure 1.7: A three-phase six-pulse TCR.

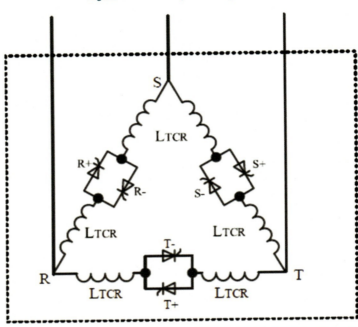

harmonic line currents flow in lines. So, we will need a single tuned filter for the fifth and seventh harmonics and a high pass filter for harmonics greater than $h = 7$ ($h = 11, 13, 17, 19$, etc.). The harmonic currents, i.e. $h = 5, 7, 11, 13$, etc., are called the characteristic harmonics. The following equations are used for calculation of tuned filter parameters.

$$Q_{cn} = \frac{I_n/n}{\sum_{m=1}^{\infty} I_m/m} \times Q_c, \qquad (1.46)$$

$$C = \frac{Q_{cn}(1 - 1/n^2)}{\omega_1 V_{ph}^2}, \qquad (1.47)$$

$$L = \frac{1}{(n\omega_1)^2 C}. \qquad (1.48)$$

where Q_c is the total capacitive reactive power compensation, Q_{cn} is the required n-filter capacitive reactive power compensation, I_n is the nth harmonic current, V_{ph} is the phase voltage, and ω_1 is the fundamental frequency (rad/s). The single tuned filter and high pass filter, which is parallel with the TCR, is depicted in Figure 1.8.

Figure 1.8: The single tuned filter and high pass filter parallel with the TCR.

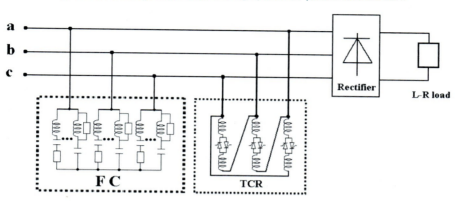

For high pass filter, R, is calculated by the equation

$$R = \frac{1}{\sqrt{d}} n\omega_1 L. \tag{1.49}$$

Typically, in practical scenarios, the value of d falls within the range of 0.5 to 1.

1.3 Static and Dynamic Equalization for Series Thyristors

At present, large thyristors on the market are capable of blocking voltages ranging from 4 to 9 kV and conducting currents from 3 to 6 kA. As a result, in real-world scenarios, valves are often constructed using multiple thyristors connected in series to achieve the necessary blocking voltage levels for a specific power rating. In series-connected thyristors (SCRs), it is necessary to ensure equalization for both static and dynamic behavior. Although the $I-V$ and reverse recovery characteristics of SCRs from the same brand and model are similar, they are not identical due to practical manufacturing limitations. As a result, series-connected SCRs will not share the total voltage equally, and the same leakage current will result in different blocking voltages. Additionally, the turn-on and turn-off behaviors of these SCRs will vary. For static equalization, resistors are used, functioning similarly to how they do for series-connected capacitors, as shown in Figure 1.9.

Figure 1.9: Adding resistors for static equalization.

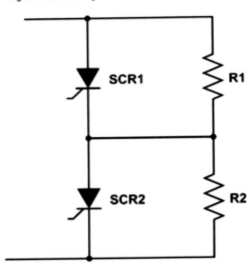

Selecting resistors involves considering the maximum allowed blocking voltage and leakage current across each SCR. The current flowing through the resistors should be sufficiently higher than the leakage currents to ensure that the leakage effects can be neglected. For dynamic equalization, a simple RC network is typically effective. However, since there is already a resistor across the SCR, adding a parallel capacitor will suffice, as illustrated in Figure 1.10.

To further enhance the circuit, a resistor can be added in series with the capacitor. This addition limits the di/dt during the capacitor discharge when the SCR turns on, protecting the SCR from excessive current. This setup is illustrated in Figure 1.11.

This RC network is incorporated to equalize the reverse recovery of the SCRs, ensuring that they do not turn on or off at different times. The additional resistance (Rc1 or Rc2) will influence the charging time of the parallel capacitors. To reduce the charging time, a fast diode can be added in parallel with these resistances. This allows for quicker charging through the diode and slower, safer discharging through the resistor, protecting the SCR. This setup is shown in Figure 1.12.

The circuit shown in Figure 1.12 primarily addresses issues related to non-synced turn-off (reverse-recovery), but it also helps mitigate problems related to non-synced turn-on. Consider the circuit in Figure 1.13. Assume the SCRs are in

Figure 1.10: Adding simple RC for dynamic equalization.

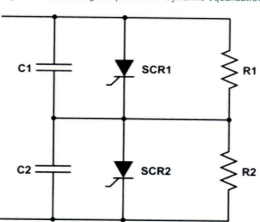

Figure 1.11: Adding a series capacitor to limit di/dt during capacitor discharge.

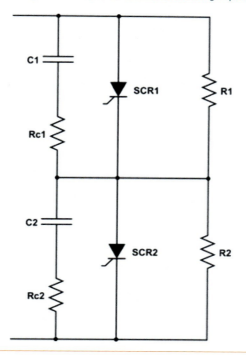

Figure 1.12: Adding a diode in parallel with resistor to charge up the capacitor faster.

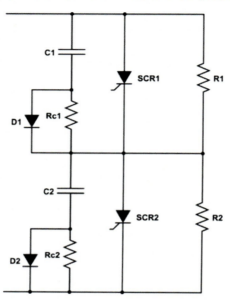

Figure 1.13: Series SCRs with static and dynamic equalizers.

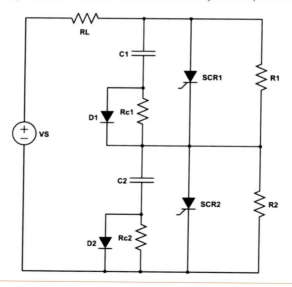

a forward blocking state (anode voltage is greater than or equal to cathode voltage, with no gate pulses applied). In this scenario, the blocking voltages across the SCRs will be half the input voltage, assisted by static equalizer resistors. If there is a non-synced firing and SCR1 is triggered first, the voltage across the "late-triggered" SCR (SCR2) will begin to rise, with a time constant determined by the load resistance (RL) and the parallel capacitance (C2), neglecting factors like SCR2's leakage and the parallel diode across Rc2. The firing delay should be shorter than this time constant to keep the voltage rise across SCR2 as low as possible. If you cannot control the firing delay, you can increase the time constant by increasing the capacitance, which will slow the voltage rise across SCR2.

2

Controller Design and Simulation of the SVC

2.1 Introduction

In the realm of modern power systems, maintaining stability and enhancing power quality are paramount objectives. One of the critical components employed to achieve these goals is the Static Var Compensator (SVC), a device used to provide fast-acting reactive power compensation on high-voltage electricity transmission networks. This chapter delves into the intricate process of designing controllers for SVCs and simulating their performance using Simulink, a versatile and powerful tool for modeling, simulating, and analyzing dynamic systems. The chapter begins with a brief overview of the fundamental principles of SVC operation and its role in power system stability and voltage regulation. Following this, it outlines the theoretical underpinnings and control strategies essential for the effective functioning of SVCs. The design of controllers for SVCs involves complex dynamics and requires a deep understanding of both control theory and power system behavior. Simulink provides an intuitive graphical interface for building and simulating models, making it an ideal platform for developing and testing SVC controllers. This chapter guides readers through the step-by-step process of creating a Simulink model of an SVC, incorporating various control strategies, and analyzing their performance under different operating conditions. Emphasis is placed on practical implementation, with detailed examples and simulations that illustrate the impact of different controller designs on system stability and performance. By the end of this chapter, readers will have a comprehensive understanding of the methodologies involved in designing and simulating SVC controllers. They will gain hands-on experience with Simulink, enabling them to apply these techniques to real-world power system scenarios, thereby contributing to the development of more robust and efficient electrical networks.

2.2 Application of Instantaneous Reactive Power Theory

The prerequisite of dynamic compensation is that the required voltage and current signals are detected out quickly and accurately. Suppose the three-phase line to line voltages to be v_{ab}, v_{bc}, v_{ca}, the three-phase source currents to be i_a, i_b, i_c, and the TCR currents to be i_{Ta}, i_{Tb}, i_{Tc}. The three-phase voltages are expressed as

$$\begin{bmatrix} v_{ab} \\ v_{bc} \\ v_{ca} \end{bmatrix} = \begin{bmatrix} V_m\sin(\omega t) \\ V_m\sin(\omega t - 2\pi/3) \\ V_m\sin(\omega t + 2\pi/3) \end{bmatrix}. \tag{2.1}$$

Here, V_m is the peak value of the voltage.

With converting equation (2.1) to α–β coordinates, we will have

$$\begin{bmatrix} v_\alpha \\ v_\beta \end{bmatrix} = \sqrt{\frac{3}{2}}V_m \begin{bmatrix} \sin(\omega t) \\ -\cos(\omega t) \end{bmatrix}. \tag{2.2}$$

According to the instantaneous reactive power theory, we can get

$$\begin{bmatrix} p \\ q \end{bmatrix} = \sqrt{\frac{3}{2}}V_m \begin{bmatrix} \sin(\omega t) & -\cos(\omega t) \\ -\cos(\omega t) & -\sin(\omega t) \end{bmatrix} \begin{bmatrix} i_\alpha \\ i_\beta \end{bmatrix}, \tag{2.3}$$

$$\begin{bmatrix} i_p \\ i_q \end{bmatrix} = \begin{bmatrix} \sin(\omega t) & -\cos(\omega t) \\ -\cos(\omega t) & -\sin(\omega t) \end{bmatrix} \begin{bmatrix} i_\alpha \\ i_\beta \end{bmatrix}. \tag{2.4}$$

The α–β conversion of the three-phase currents, i_a, i_b, i_c, is given as

$$\begin{bmatrix} i_\alpha \\ i_\beta \end{bmatrix} = \sqrt{\frac{2}{3}} \begin{bmatrix} 1 & -1/2 & -1/2 \\ 0 & \sqrt{3}/2 & -\sqrt{3}/2 \end{bmatrix} \begin{bmatrix} i_a \\ i_b \\ i_c \end{bmatrix}. \tag{2.5}$$

By substituting equation (2.5) into equation (2.4), we obtain

$$\begin{bmatrix} i_p \\ i_q \end{bmatrix} = \sqrt{\frac{2}{3}} \begin{bmatrix} \sin(\omega t) & \sin(\omega t - 2\pi/3) & \sin(\omega t + 2\pi/3) \\ -\cos(\omega t) & -\cos(\omega t - 2\pi/3) & -\cos(\omega t + 2\pi/3) \end{bmatrix} \begin{bmatrix} i_a \\ i_b \\ i_c \end{bmatrix}. \tag{2.6}$$

We suppose

$$I_{TCR} \text{ and } I_S = i_q. \tag{2.7}$$

We can obtain the current of TCR and source current as

$$I_{TCR} = -\sqrt{\frac{2}{3}} \left[i_{Ta} \cos(\omega t) + i_{Tb} \cos(\omega t - 2\pi/3) + i_{Tc} \cos(\omega t + 2\pi/3) \right], \tag{2.8}$$

$$I_S = -\sqrt{\frac{2}{3}} \left[i_a \cos(\omega t) + i_b \cos(\omega t - 2\pi/3) + i_c \cos(\omega t + 2\pi/3) \right]. \tag{2.9}$$

Also, we suppose

$$V_{Line} = v_p. \tag{2.10}$$

Then, we can write the line voltage as

$$V_{Line} = \sqrt{\frac{2}{3}} \left[v_{ab} \sin(\omega t) + v_{bc} \sin(\omega t - 2\pi/3) + v_{ca} \sin(\omega t + 2\pi/3) \right]. \tag{2.11}$$

In equations (2.8), (2.9), and (2.11), I_{TCR}, I_S, and V_{Line} are DC quantities corresponding to the fundamental components of three-phase currents and voltage respectively. The goal of the control system is to maintain the voltage value of the power grid constant when load disturbance occurs and to make sure the power factor of the system is greater than 0.95. The control strategy of SVC is shown in Figure 2.1.

Figure 2.1: The control strategy of the SVC.

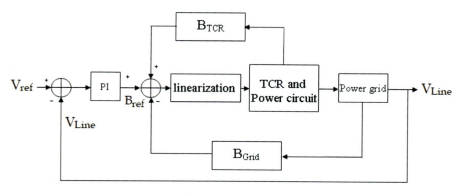

In Figure 2.1, B_{TCR} and B_{Grid} are defined as

$$B_{TCR} = \frac{I_{TCR}}{V_{Line}}, \qquad (2.12)$$

$$B_{Grid} = \frac{I_S}{V_{Line}}. \qquad (2.13)$$

According to the control requirements, the voltage-closed loop should lie in the outer-loop to make the voltage constant, and the inner loop is an admittance of the compensation loop, which aims to increase the dynamic response rate of the system to load disturbance. When reactive power admittance changed, according to the quantity detected, TCR computes out the value of α to offset it. At the same time, when the active power admittance of the load also changes, the PI regulator generates a given value of admittance to assure the grid voltage constant and the power factor ranges from 0.95 to 1 in the system. The control part also includes non-linear segment and a six-pulse generator. According to Figure 2.4, the relationship between fundamental component of the current within the TCR and α is non-linear, so the linearization segment was brought in to make the output of PI regulator consistent with I_1. The lookup table model of Simulink is adopted to fulfill the linearization in this design. The Simulink model of control section is depicted in Figure 2.2.

Figure 2.2: Control section of the SVC in Simulink.

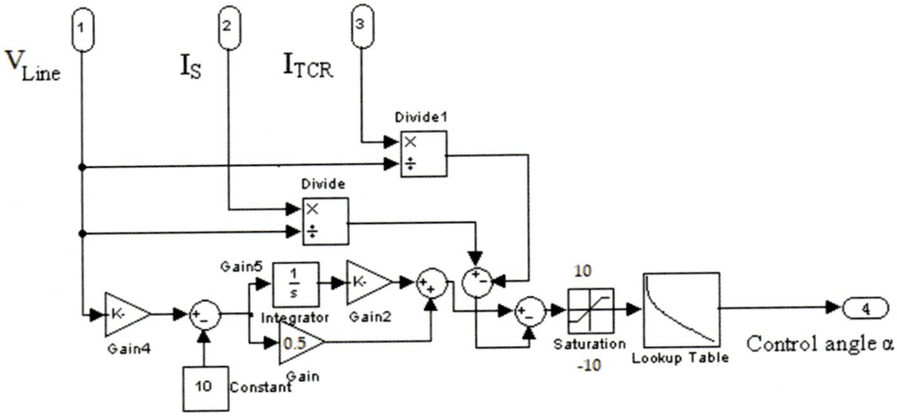

The six-pulse generator block is used to trigger the TCR and its model in Simulink is illustrated in Figure 2.3.

Figure 2.3: The block of the TCR and the six-pulse generator.

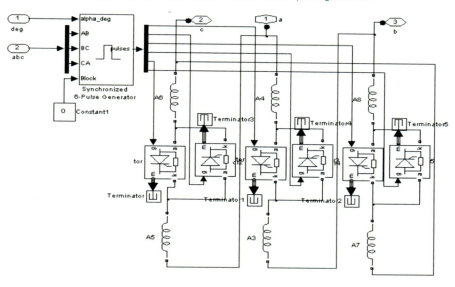

2.3 SVC Controller Simulation in Simulink

In this section, we will simulate the SVC controller using Simulink. All simulation files are available in [5]. The whole three-phase system with a connected SVC and its controller, which is parallel to a nonlinear load, is shown in Figure 2.4.

The three-phase source block parameters are depicted in Figure 2.5.

The Yg-connected series R–L load has the following parameters

$$R = 100 \ \Omega, \ L = 100 \ \text{mH}. \tag{2.14}$$

Also, the three-phase diode rectifier load parameters are as below

$$R = 10 \ \Omega, \ L = 10 \ \text{mH}. \tag{2.15}$$

The delta-connected TCR has the following inductance value for each of six reactors

$$L = 10 \ \text{mH}. \tag{2.16}$$

Figure 2.4: The three-phase system with a connected SVC.

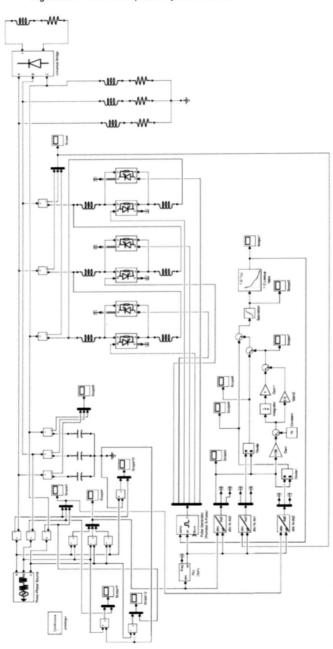

Figure 2.5: The three-phase source block parameters.

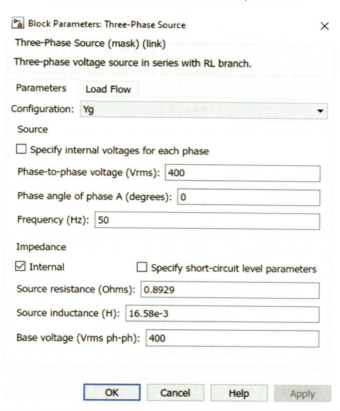

As we know, the inductor is in series with capacitor within a harmonic filter (HF) branch of the SVC. To filter out the specific harmonics, the L and C should be resonated at a giving frequency. At the same time, for the fundamental frequency wave, the reactive power provided by capacitors is greater than that consumed by inductors, hence, the total reactive power is capacitive in an HF branch at fundamental frequency. For simplicity, we replace all HFs with a fixed capacitor (FC). The Yg-connected FC has the following capacitance:

$$C = 20 \ \mu\text{F}. \tag{2.17}$$

The three-phase PLL block parameters and the abc to dq0 transformation block parameters are illustrated in Figures 2.6 and 2.7 respectively. In addition, the thyristor six-pulse generator block parameters are shown in Figure 2.8.

Figure 2.6: The three-phase PLL block parameters.

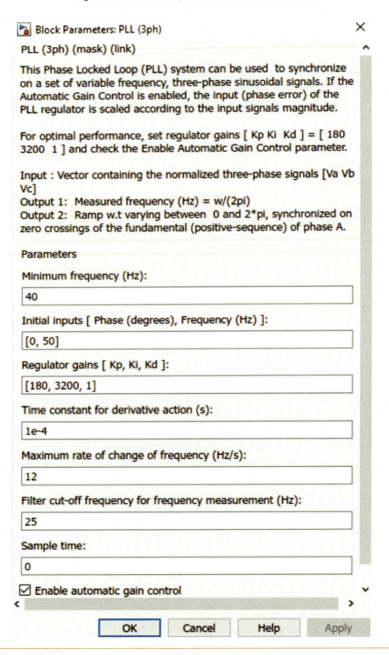

Block Parameters: PLL (3ph)   ✕

PLL (3ph) (mask) (link)

This Phase Locked Loop (PLL) system can be used to synchronize on a set of variable frequency, three-phase sinusoidal signals. If the Automatic Gain Control is enabled, the input (phase error) of the PLL regulator is scaled according to the input signals magnitude.

For optimal performance, set regulator gains [Kp Ki Kd] = [180 3200 1] and check the Enable Automatic Gain Control parameter.

Input : Vector containing the normalized three-phase signals [Va Vb Vc]
Output 1: Measured frequency (Hz) = w/(2pi)
Output 2: Ramp w.t varying between 0 and 2*pi, synchronized on zero crossings of the fundamental (positive-sequence) of phase A.

Parameters

Minimum frequency (Hz):

40

Initial inputs [Phase (degrees), Frequency (Hz)]:

[0, 50]

Regulator gains [Kp, Ki, Kd]:

[180, 3200, 1]

Time constant for derivative action (s):

1e-4

Maximum rate of change of frequency (Hz/s):

12

Filter cut-off frequency for frequency measurement (Hz):

25

Sample time:

0

☑ Enable automatic gain control

OK   Cancel   Help   Apply

Figure 2.7: The abc to dq0 transformation block parameters.

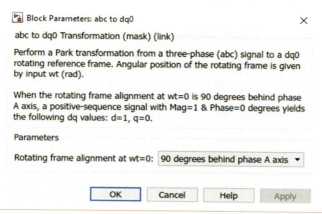

Figure 2.8: The thyristor six-pulse generator block parameters.

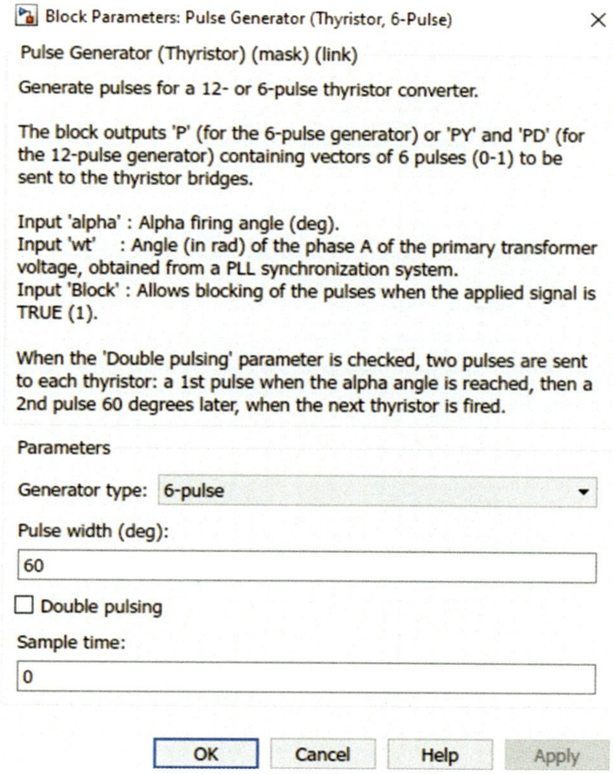

The saturation block parameters are depicted in Figure 2.9. Also, the 1-D lookup table block parameters are illustrated in Figure 2.10.

Figure 2.9: The saturation block parameters.

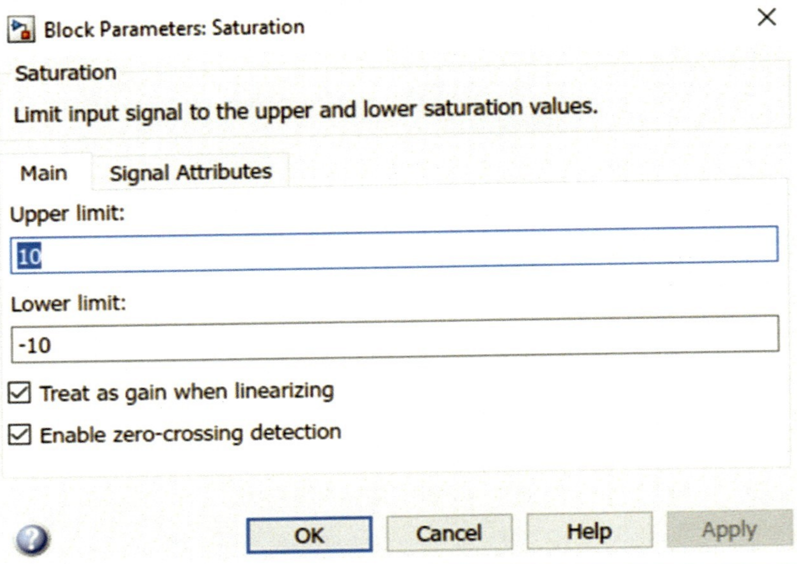

Figure 2.10: The 1-D lookup table block parameters.

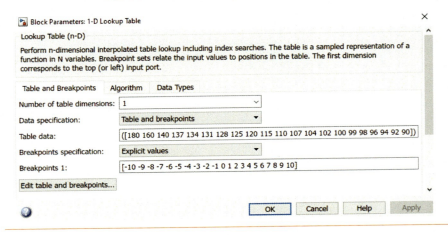

Before running the three-phase system with a connected SVC in Figure 2.4, we want to observe the line voltage of currents in the same system without the SVC. The three-phase system without the SVC is shown in Figure 2.11.

Figure 2.11: The three-phase system without the SVC.

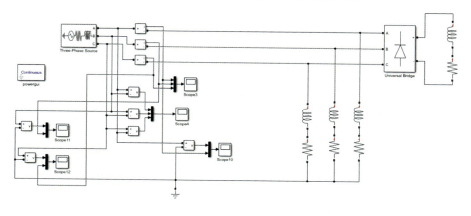

The line voltage and current of phase "a" without the SVC is depicted in Figure 2.12.

Figure 2.12: The line voltage and current of phase "a" without the SVC.

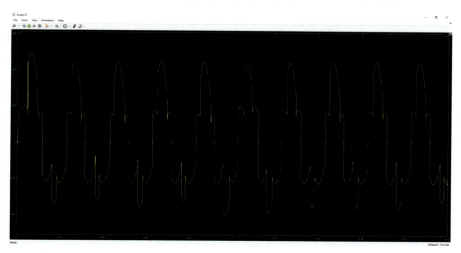

If we run the three-phase system with a connected SVC in Figure 2.4, the line voltage and current of phase "a" are displayed on the scope, as you can see in Figure 2.13.

Figure 2.13: The line voltage and current of phase "a" with SVC.

As you can see in Figure 2.13, by applying the SVC the voltage and current unbalances as well as the system power factor are improved significantly. In the next chapter, we are going to discretize this continuous time system to prepare it for code generation.

3

Discretization and Code Generation of an SVC

3.1 Introduction

As the complexity and scale of modern power systems continue to grow, the need for advanced tools and techniques to enhance system stability and efficiency becomes increasingly critical. The Static Var Compensator (SVC) is a pivotal device in this context, used to regulate voltage and improve the power quality of electrical networks. To effectively implement SVCs in real-time systems, the processes of discretization and automatic code generation are essential. This chapter focuses on these processes within the Simulink environment, providing a thorough exploration of how continuous-time SVC models can be converted into discrete-time implementations and subsequently transformed into deployable code. The chapter begins by outlining the fundamental concepts of discretization, explaining the necessity of converting continuous-time models to discrete-time models for digital controller implementation. It discusses various discretization techniques, highlighting their impact on system performance and accuracy. Readers will gain insights into the challenges and considerations involved in the discretization process, including sampling rates, quantization effects, and stability issues. Following the theoretical background, the chapter transitions to a practical guide on using Simulink for discretizing SVC models. It details the step-by-step procedures for transforming continuous-time models into discrete equivalents within Simulink, utilizing built-in tools and functions. Emphasis is placed on ensuring that the discretized models accurately reflect the dynamics of the original system while being suitable for digital implementation. The latter part of the chapter is dedicated to code generation, a crucial step in bringing Simulink models to life in real-time applications. Readers will learn how to leverage Simulink's capabilities to automatically generate efficient, executable code from their discrete-time SVC models. The chapter covers the configuration and customization of code generation settings, the integration of generated code with real-time hardware, and the verification and validation of the implementation. By the end of this chapter, readers will have a comprehensive understanding of the discretization process and its importance in digital controller design for SVCs. They will also be equipped with practical skills in using Simulink for both discretization and automatic code generation, empowering them to implement sophisticated SVC controllers in real-world power system applications. This knowledge will be invaluable for engineers and researchers aiming to enhance the performance and reliability of modern electrical networks through advanced control strategies and real-time digital implementations.

3.2 Discretization of an SVC in Simulink

In this section, we are going to discretize the SVC designed with Simulink as you can see in Figure 2.4. All simulation files are available in [5]. To begin discretizing, we first change the simulation type of powergui block parameters from continuous to discrete and the sample time to 10 μs as shown in Figure 3.1.

Figure 3.1: The powergui block parameters.

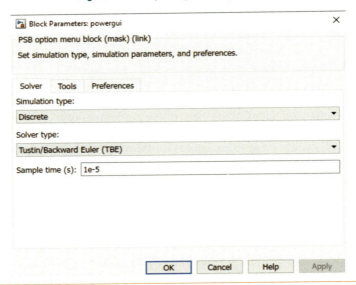

Since the three-phase PLL and thyristor six-pulse generator in Figure 2.4, cannot be converted to the C code using a MATLAB embedded coder, we should design them in the discrete time domain. The designed subsystem of the PLL is depicted in Figure 3.2.

Figure 3.2: The designed subsystem of the PLL.

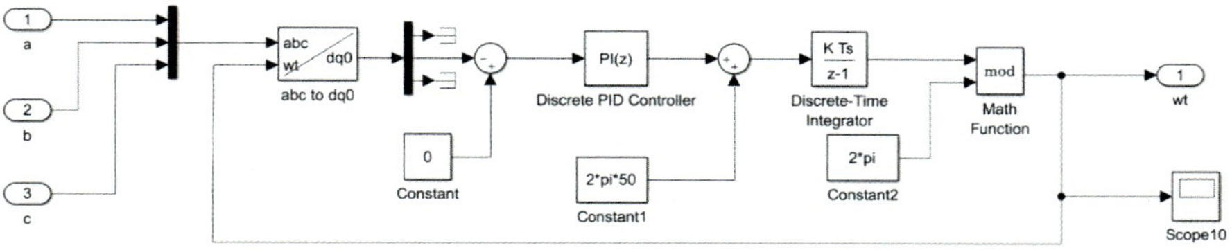

The discrete PI controller and discrete-time integrator block parameters are illustrated in Figures 3.3 and 3.4, respectively.

Figure 3.3: The discrete PI controller block parameters.

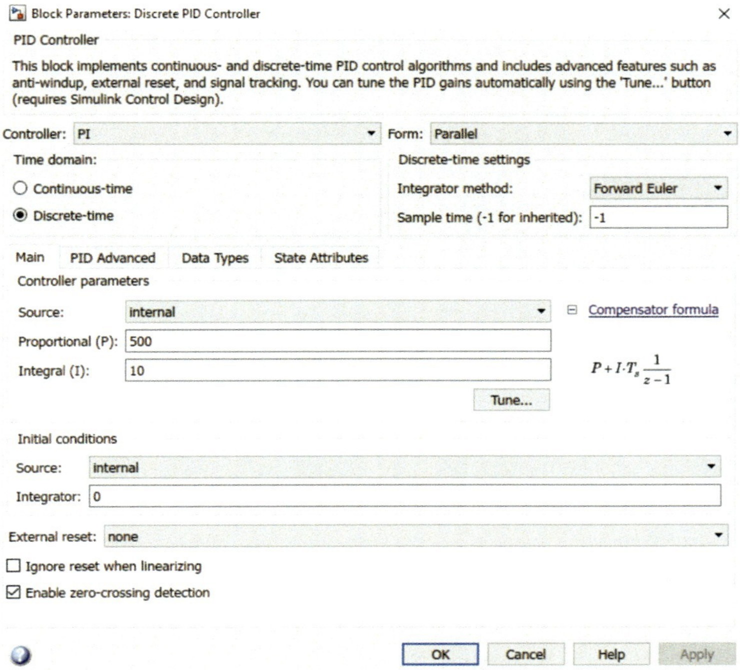

Figure 3.4: The discrete-time integrator block parameters.

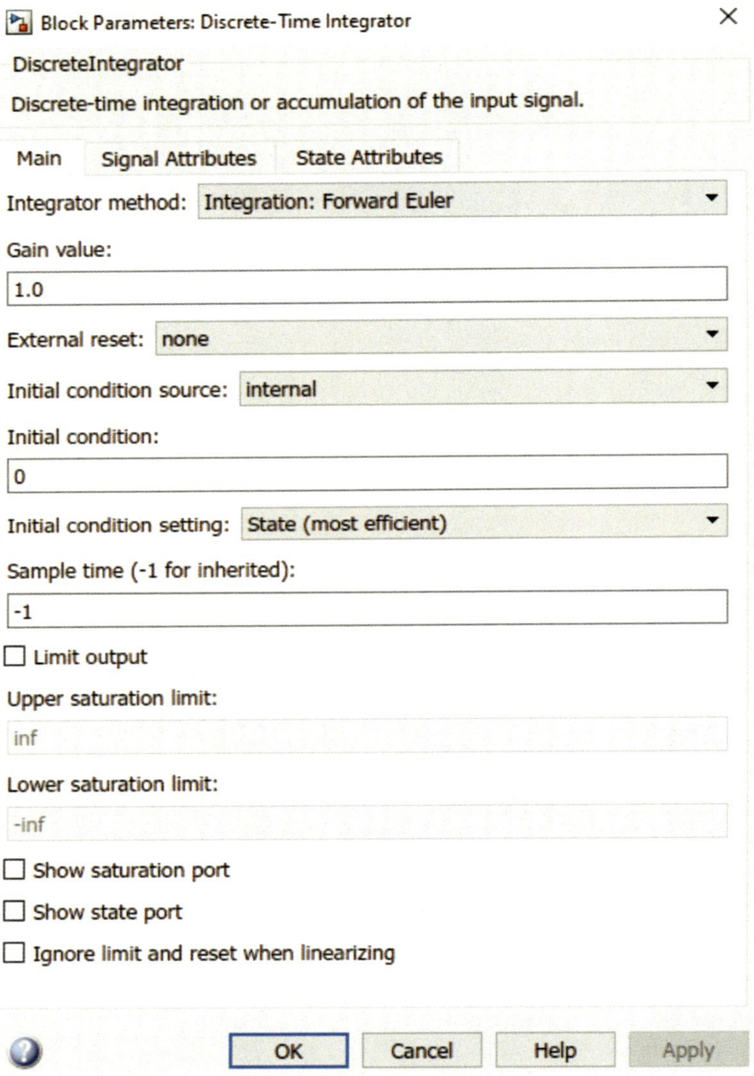

Block Parameters: Discrete-Time Integrator ✕

DiscreteIntegrator

Discrete-time integration or accumulation of the input signal.

Main   Signal Attributes   State Attributes

Integrator method: Integration: Forward Euler ▼

Gain value:

```
1.0
```

External reset: none ▼

Initial condition source: internal ▼

Initial condition:

```
0
```

Initial condition setting: State (most efficient) ▼

Sample time (-1 for inherited):

```
-1
```

☐ Limit output

Upper saturation limit:

```
inf
```

Lower saturation limit:

```
-inf
```

☐ Show saturation port

☐ Show state port

☐ Ignore limit and reset when linearizing

OK   Cancel   Help   Apply

The six-pulse generator subsystem (6pulse_gen) is shown in Figure 3.5.

The rate transition and data type conversion block parameters are depicted in Figures 3.6 and 3.7, respectively.

Figure 3.5: The six-pulse generator subsystem (6pulse_gen).

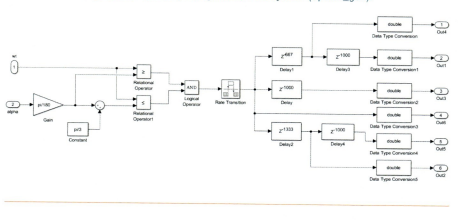

Figure 3.6: The rate transition block parameters.

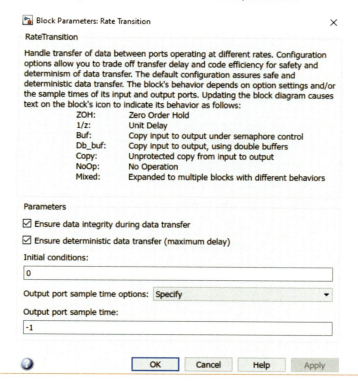

Figure 3.7: The data type conversion block parameters.

Figure 3.7: The data type conversion block parameters.

📓 Block Parameters: Data Type Conversion   ✕

Data Type Conversion

Convert the input to the data type and scaling of the output.

The conversion has two possible goals. One goal is to have the Real World Values of the input and the output be equal. The other goal is to have the Stored Integer Values of the input and the output be equal. Overflows and quantization errors can prevent the goal from being fully achieved.

Parameters

Output minimum: Output maximum:

[ ]   []

Output data type: double   ⌄   >>

☐ Lock output data type setting against changes by the fixed-point tools

Input and output to have equal: Real World Value (RWV)   ▾

Integer rounding mode: Floor   ▾

☐ Saturate on integer overflow

?   OK   Cancel   Help   Apply

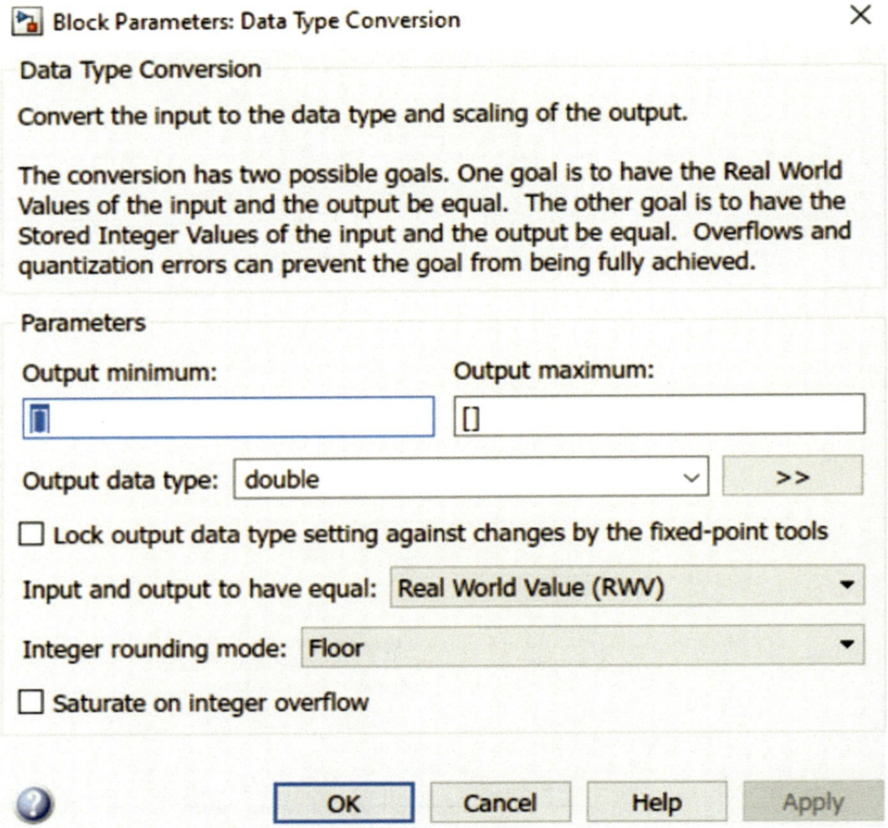

The whole three-phase system with the connected SVC in the discrete-time domain is illustrated in Figure 3.8.

In this case, the TCR inductance value of each of the six reactors is

$$L = 100 \text{ mH}. \tag{3.1}$$

We want to insert all controller blocks inside a subsystem called SVC_Controller. To do that we select all the control blocks we want to put inside the subsystem, right click and then select the Create Subsystem from Selection (Ctrl+G), as you can see in Figure 3.9.

Figure 3.8: Discretized three-phase system with the connected SVC.

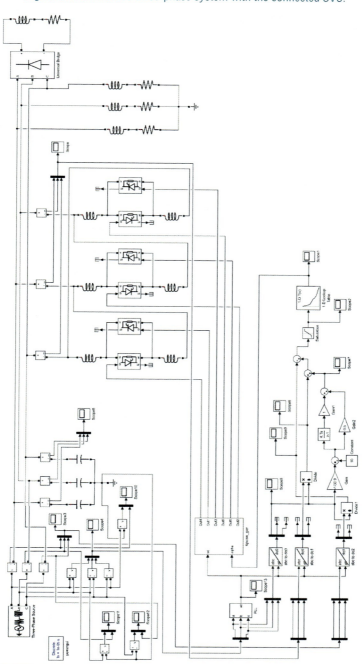

Figure 3.9: Selecting the Create Subsystem from Selection (Ctrl+G).

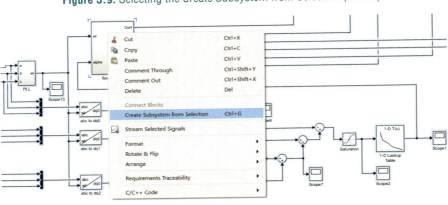

The whole SVC connected three-phase system with the SVC_Controller subsystem is shown in Figure 3.10.

Figure 3.10: SVC connected three-phase system with the SVC_Controller subsystem.

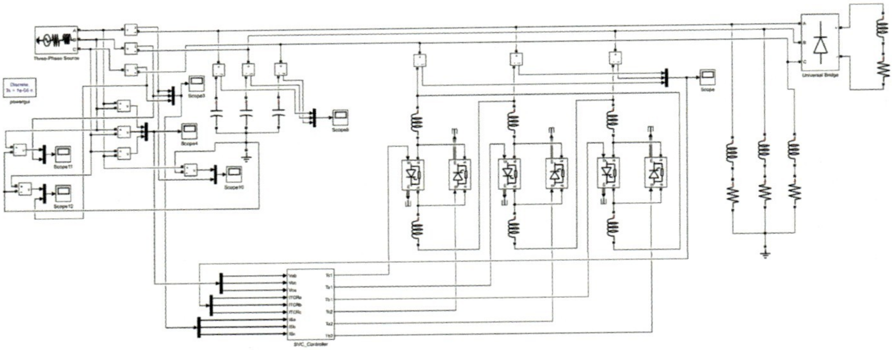

The SVC_Controller subsystem block diagram is depicted in Figure 3.11.

If we run the discretized three-phase system with a connected SVC in Figure 3.10, the line voltage and current of phase "a" are displayed on the scope, as you can see in Figure 3.12.

As you can see in Figure 3.12, the line voltage and current of the phase "a" waveform with discretized SVC control is more similar to the continuous-time analysis, as you can see in Figure 2.13.

Figure 3.11: The SVC_Controller subsystem block diagram.

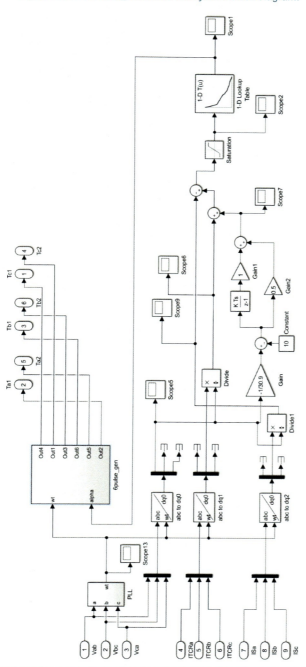

Figure 3.12: The line voltage and current of phase "a" with discretized SVC control.

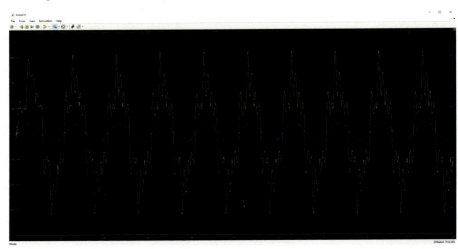

3.3 Code Generation for Discretized SVC Control

All the generated codes can be found in [5], so in order to prepare the code generation of the SVC connected three-phase system, as seen in Figure 3.10, we select the model configuration parameters icon, as illustrated in Figure 3.13.

Figure 3.13: Selecting the model configuration parameters icon.

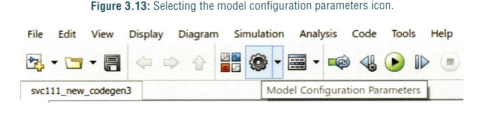

Then, in the pop-up configuration parameters window, we set the solver options type as Fixed-step, as shown in Figure 3.14.

In the Code Generation section, we click on the Browse... button and select Embedded Coder (ert.tlc) as the system target file, then we click on the Apply and OK buttons, as depicted in Figure 3.15.

Figure 3.14: Setting the solver options type as Fixed-step.

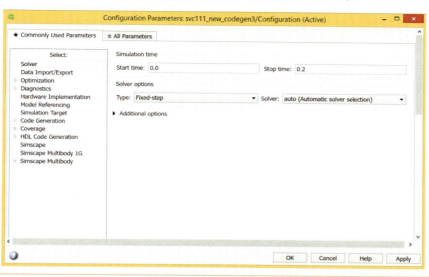

Figure 3.15: Selecting Embedded Coder (ert.tlc) as the system target file.

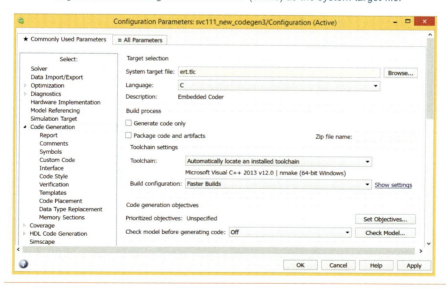

We right click on the subsystem "SVC_Controller" and select the Block parameters (Subsystem) option, as you can see in Figure 3.16.

Figure 3.16: Selecting the Block parameters (Subsystem) option.

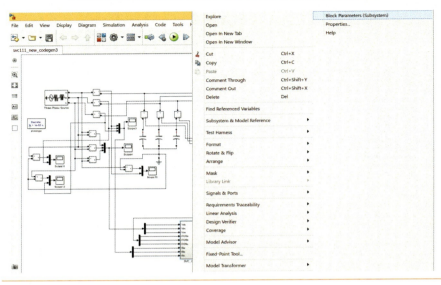

In the pop-up block parameters window we tick on the Treat as atomic unit option, then click on the Apply and OK buttons, as illustrated in Figure 3.17.

Figure 3.17: Clicking on the Treat as atomic unit option.

We right click on the subsystem "SVC_Controller" and select Subsystem & Model Reference → Convert Subsystem to → Reference Model… options, as shown in Figure 3.18.

Figure 3.18: Selecting the Reference Model… option.

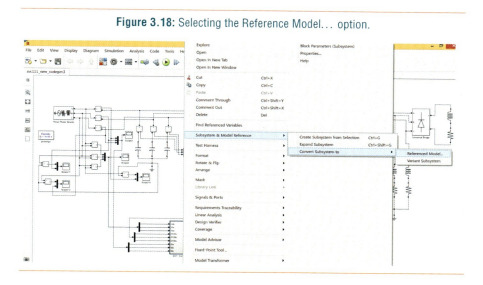

In the Model Reference Conversion Advisor window, we click on the Convert button, as depicted in Figure 3.19. The conversion of the subsystem

Figure 3.19: Clicking on the Convert button.

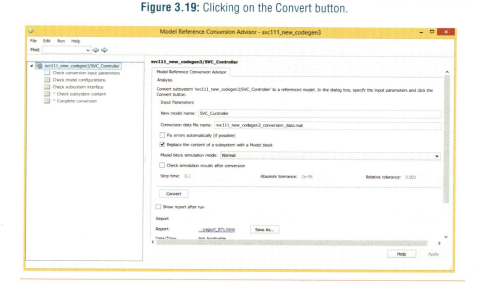

"SVC_Controller" to the reference model is done successfully, as you can see in Figures 3.20 and 3.21 respectively.

Figure 3.20: The successful conversion of the subsystem to the reference model.

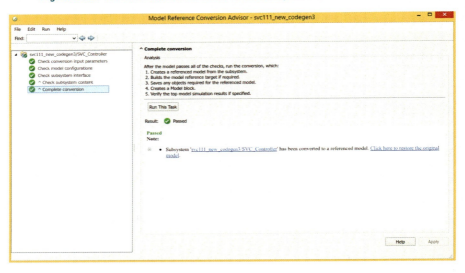

Figure 3.21: The conversion of the subsystem "SVC_Controller" to the reference model.

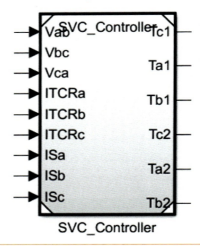

SVC_Controller

If we run the simulation again, we will get the same result on the scope as depicted in Figure 3.12. Then inside the subsystem "SVC_Controller", we can build the model by clicking on the Build Model button, as illustrated in Figure 3.22.

Figure 3.22: Clicking on the Build Model button.

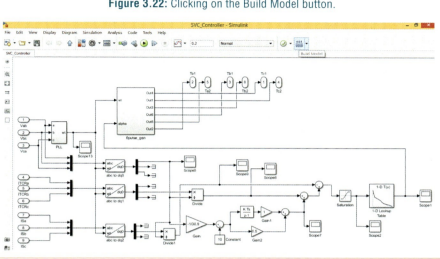

The build process is completed successfully as shown in the Diagnostic Viewer window of Figure 3.23.

Figure 3.23: Successful build process message in the Diagnostic Viewer window.

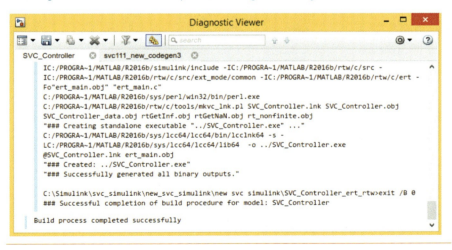

The Summary and Code Interface Report of the Code Generation Report window are depicted in Figures 3.24 and 3.25, respectively.

Figure 3.24: The Summary of Code Generation Report window.

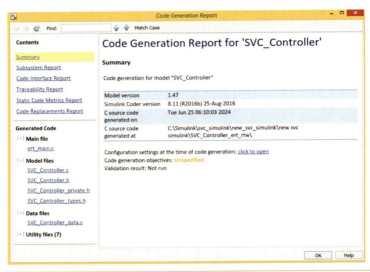

Figure 3.25: The Code Interface Report of the Code Generation Report window.

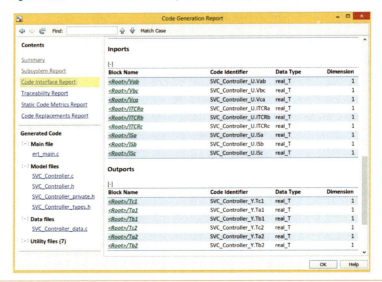

4

SVC Controller Implementation with Arduino

4.1 Introduction

As technology continues to advance at an unprecedented rate, the need for efficient and reliable control systems has become increasingly important. In the field of power electronics, the implementation of Static Voltage Compensators (SVCs) has been widely used to stabilize the voltage within power systems. These SVCs are essential in maintaining the stability and efficiency of power grids by regulating the voltage fluctuations that occur during sudden changes in load or disturbances. In this chapter, we will focus on the implementation of an SVC controller using an Arduino microcontroller, combined with the power of Simulink's code generation capabilities. By utilizing Simulink's intuitive modeling environment and Arduino's user-friendly interface, we aim to demonstrate how a powerful and precise control system can be developed with ease and efficiency. We are aware of the Arduino microcontroller and its suitability for real-time control applications. The Arduino platform offers a cost-effective and versatile solution for developing control systems, making it an ideal choice for implementing an SVC controller. Simulink is as a powerful tool for modeling and simulating control systems. With its block diagram approach and extensive library of pre-built blocks, Simulink provides a convenient way to design complex control systems and test their performance in a virtual environment. We demonstrated how Simulink can be used to model the dynamics of an SVC system and develop a controller that meets the design requirements. Furthermore, we will delve into the process of generated code from Simulink model in the previous chapter and deploying it onto the Arduino board. Simulink's code generation capabilities enable us to convert the control algorithm into executable code that can be uploaded to the Arduino, allowing us to implement the SVC controller in a real-world setting. We will provide step-by-step instructions on how to deploy the generated code onto the Arduino, ensuring a seamless transition from simulation to implementation. In conclusion, this chapter will demonstrate the powerful combination of Arduino, Simulink, and SVC control systems. By leveraging the capabilities of these tools, we can develop a robust and efficient controller that enhances the stability and reliability of power systems. Through practical examples and hands-on exercises, readers will gain valuable insights into the implementation of control systems using Arduino and Simulink, empowering them to tackle complex control challenges in the field of power electronics.

4.2 Adding Generated Codes to the Library of Arduino IDE

The generated codes in the previous chapter are saved in a folder named "SVC_Controller_ert_rtw". We copy and paste it into the directory shown in Figure 4.1.

This PC → Documents → Arduino

Figure 4.1: Copying and pasting the "SVC_Controller_ert_rtw" folder.

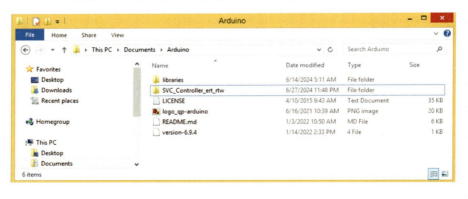

Then, we create the folders named SVC_Controller, SVC_Controller_ private, SVC_Controller_types, rtwtypes, rtw_solver, rtw_continuous, rt_ nonfinite, rtGetInf, and rtGetNaN inside the libraries folder, as depicted in Figure 4.2.

Figure 4.2: Creating some folders inside the libraries folder.

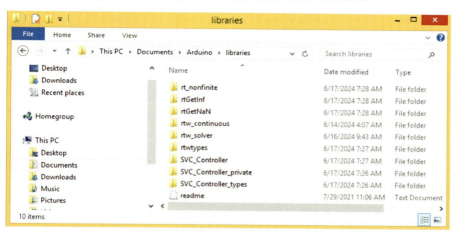

All the generated code files inside the SVC_Controller_ert_rtw folder are illustrated in Figure 4.3.

Figure 4.3: All files inside the SVC_Controller_ert_rtw folder.

We copy and paste all the header files in Figure 4.3 to the corresponding folders created in Figure 4.2. You can see that there are no header files for rtw_continuous.h and rtw_solver.h in the generated files in Figure 4.3. Therefore, you can download it from my book titled "Advanced programming with STM32 Microcontrollers" program files folder:

https://www.elektor.com/products/advanced-programming-with-stm32-microcontrollers

The copied header files inside corresponding folders are shown in Figures 4.4–4.12.

Figure 4.4: Copying and pasting the rt_nonfinite.h file.

Figure 4.5: Copying and pasting the rtGetInf.h file.

Figure 4.6: Copying and pasting the rtGetNaN.h file.

Figure 4.7: Copying and pasting the rtw_continuous.h file.

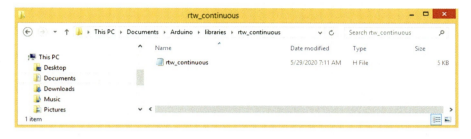

Figure 4.8: Copying and pasting the rtw_solver.h file.

Figure 4.9: Copying and pasting the rtwtypes.h file.

Figure 4.10: Copying and pasting the SVC_Controller.h file.

Figure 4.11: Copying and pasting the SVC_Controller_private.h file.

Figure 4.12: Copying and pasting the SVC_Controller_types.h file.

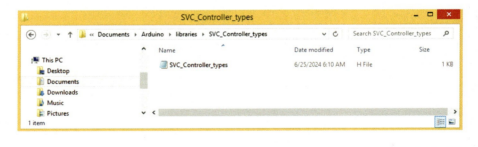

4.3 Coding SVC Controller in Arduino IDE

In this section, we will use the Arduino Mega 2560 development board to program our SVC controller as in Figure 4.13.

Figure 4.13: The Arduino Mega 2560 development board.

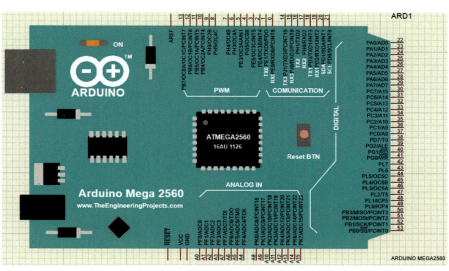

We will use the following code structure in Arduino IDE. The Arduino sketches are available in [5].

```
#include "SVC_Controller.h"
#include "SVC_Controller_private.h"
#include "SVC_Controller.h"
#include "Arduino.h"
#include <stddef.h>
#include <stdio.h>
#include "rtwtypes.h"
#include "rt_nonfinite.h"
#include "rtGetNaN.h"
#include "rtGetInf.h"
int Vab = A0;
double VabValue = 0;

int Vbc = A1;
double VbcValue = 0;

int Vca = A2;
double VcaValue = 0;

int ITCRa = A3;
double ITCRaValue = 0;

int ITCRb = A4;
```

```
double ITCRbValue = 0;

int ITCRc = A5;
double ITCRcValue = 0;

int ISa = A6;
double ISaValue = 0;

int ISb = A7;
double ISbValue = 0;

int ISc = A8;
double IScValue = 0;

int Ta1 = 4;
double Ta1Val = 0;

int Tb1 = 5;
double Tb1Val = 0;
int Tc1 = 6;
double Tc1Val = 0;

int Ta2 = 7;
double Ta2Val = 0;
int Tb2 = 8;
double Tb2Val = 0;

int Tc2 = 9;
double Tc2Val = 0;

//SVC_Controller_data.c

//rt_nonfinite.c

//rtGetInf.c

//rtGetNaN.c

void setup() {
  // put your setup code here, to run once:

  Serial.begin(9600);
  pinMode(Vab,INPUT);
  pinMode(Vbc,INPUT);
  pinMode(Vca,INPUT);
  pinMode(ITCRa,INPUT);
  pinMode(ITCRb,INPUT);
  pinMode(ITCRc,INPUT);
  pinMode(ISa,INPUT);
  pinMode(ISb,INPUT);
  pinMode(ISc,INPUT);
  pinMode(Ta1,OUTPUT);
  pinMode(Tb1,OUTPUT);
  pinMode(Tc1,OUTPUT);
  pinMode(Ta2,OUTPUT);
```

```
    pinMode(Tb2,OUTPUT);
    pinMode(Tc2,OUTPUT);

    SVC_Controller_initialize();

}

void loop() {
    // put your main code here, to run repeatedly:
    VabValue = analogRead(Vab);
    VabValue = (VabValue/1023-2.5)*125;
    SVC_Controller_U.Vab = VabValue;

    VbcValue = analogRead(Vbc);
    VbcValue = (VabValue/1023-2.5)*125;
    SVC_Controller_U.Vbc = VbcValue;

    VcaValue = analogRead(Vca);
    VcaValue = (VcaValue/1023-2.5)*125;
    SVC_Controller_U.Vca = VcaValue;

    ITCRaValue = analogRead(ITCRa);
    ITCRaValue = (ITCRaValue/1023-2.5)*4;
    SVC_Controller_U.ITCRa = ITCRaValue;

    ITCRbValue = analogRead(ITCRb);
    ITCRbValue = (ITCRbValue/1023-2.5)*4;
    SVC_Controller_U.ITCRb = ITCRbValue;

    ITCRcValue = analogRead(ITCRc);
    ITCRcValue = (ITCRcValue/1023-2.5)*4;
    SVC_Controller_U.ITCRc = ITCRcValue;

    ISaValue = analogRead(ISa);
    ISaValue = (ISaValue/1023-2.5)*16;
    SVC_Controller_U.ISa = ISaValue;

    ISbValue = analogRead(ISb);
    ISbValue = (ISbValue/1023-2.5)*16;
    SVC_Controller_U.ISb = ISbValue;

    IScValue = analogRead(ISc);
    IScValue = (IScValue/1023-2.5)*16;
    SVC_Controller_U.ISc = IScValue;

    SVC_Controller_step();

    Ta1Val = 255*SVC_Controller_Y.Ta1;
    analogWrite(Ta1,Ta1Val);

    Tb1Val = 255*SVC_Controller_Y.Tb1;
    analogWrite(Tb1,Tb1Val);

    Tc1Val = 255*SVC_Controller_Y.Tc1;
    analogWrite(Tc1,Tc1Val);
```

```
Ta2Val = 255*SVC_Controller_Y.Ta2;
analogWrite(Ta2,Ta2Val);

Tb2Val = 255*SVC_Controller_Y.Tb2;
analogWrite(Tb2,Tb2Val);

Tc2Val = 255*SVC_Controller_Y.Tc2;
analogWrite(Tc2,Tc2Val);

delayMicroseconds(10);

}
//SVC_Controller.c
```

As highlighted in the code, we should put the codes inside the SVC_Controller.c file after the loop function; however, we should put the codes inside the SVC_Controller_data.c, rt_nonfinite.c, rtGetInf, and rtGetNaN files before the setup function. Therefore, the complete code for our SVC controller will be:

```
#include "SVC_Controller.h"
#include "SVC_Controller_private.h"
#include "SVC_Controller.h"
#include "Arduino.h"
#include <stddef.h>
#include <stdio.h>
#include "rtwtypes.h"
#include "rt_nonfinite.h"
#include "rtGetNaN.h"
#include "rtGetInf.h"

int Vab = A0;
double VabValue = 0;

int Vbc = A1;
double VbcValue = 0;

int Vca = A2;
double VcaValue = 0;

int ITCRa = A3;
double ITCRaValue = 0;

int ITCRb = A4;
double ITCRbValue = 0;

int ITCRc = A5;
double ITCRcValue = 0;

int ISa = A6;
double ISaValue = 0;
```

```
int ISb = A7;
double ISbValue = 0;

int ISc = A8;
double IScValue = 0;

int Ta1 = 4;
double Ta1Val = 0;
int Tb1 = 5;
double Tb1Val = 0;

int Tc1 = 6;
double Tc1Val = 0;

int Ta2 = 7;
double Ta2Val = 0;

int Tb2 = 8;
double Tb2Val = 0;

int Tc2 = 9;
double Tc2Val = 0;

/*
 * File: SVC_Controller_data.c
 *
 * Code generated for Simulink model 'SVC_Controller'.
 *
 * Model version              : 1.47
 * Simulink Coder version     : 8.11 (R2016b) 25-Aug-2016
 * C/C++ source code generated on : Tue Jun 25 06:10:03 2024
 *
 * Target selection: ert.tlc
 * Embedded hardware selection: Intel->x86-64 (Windows64)
 * Code generation objectives: Unspecified
 * Validation result: Not run
 */

/* Invariant block signals (auto storage) */
const ConstB_SVC_Controller_T SVC_Controller_ConstB = {
  0U,                  /* '<S28>/Compare' */
  1U,                  /* '<S29>/Compare' */
  0U,                  /* '<S16>/Compare' */
  1U,                  /* '<S17>/Compare' */
  0U,                  /* '<S22>/Compare' */
  1U,                  /* '<S23>/Compare' */
  0U,                  /* '<S10>/Compare' */
  1U                   /* '<S11>/Compare' */
};

/* Constant parameters (auto storage) */
const ConstP_SVC_Controller_T SVC_Controller_ConstP = {
  /* Pooled Parameter (Expression: [ 1   -1/2  -1/2; 0  sqrt(3)/2  -sqrt(3)/2; 1/2
  1/2  1/2 ] )
```

```
 * Referenced by:
 *   '<S15>/Gain3'
 *   '<S21>/Gain3'
 *  '<S27>/Gain3'
 *   '<S9>/Gain3'
 */
{ 1.0, 0.0, 0.5, -0.5, 0.8660254037844386, 0.5, -0.5, -0.8660254037844386,
  0.5
},

 /* Expression: ([180 160 140 137 134 131 128 125 120 115 110 107 104 102
  100 99 98 96 94 92 90])
  * Referenced by: '<Root>/1-D Lookup Table'
  */
{ 180.0, 160.0, 140.0, 137.0, 134.0, 131.0, 128.0, 125.0, 120.0, 115.0, 110.0,
  107.0, 104.0, 102.0, 100.0, 99.0, 98.0, 96.0, 94.0, 92.0, 90.0 },

 /* Expression: [-10 -9 -8 -7 -6 -5 -4 -3 -2 -1 0 1 2 3 4 5 6 7 8 9 10]
  * Referenced by: '<Root>/1-D Lookup Table'
  */
{ -10.0, -9.0, -8.0, -7.0, -6.0, -5.0, -4.0, -3.0, -2.0, -1.0, 0.0, 1.0, 2.0,
  3.0, 4.0, 5.0, 6.0, 7.0, 8.0, 9.0, 10.0 }
};

/*
 * File trailer for generated code.
 *
 * [EOF]
 */


/*
 * File: rt_nonfinite.c
 *
 * Code generated for Simulink model 'SVC_Controller'.
 *
 * Model version              : 1.47
 * Simulink Coder version     : 8.11 (R2016b) 25-Aug-2016
 * C/C++ source code generated on : Tue Jun 25 06:10:03 2024
 *
 * Target selection: ert.tlc
 * Embedded hardware selection: Intel->x86-64 (Windows64)
 * Code generation objectives: Unspecified
 * Validation result: Not run
 */

/*
 * Abstract:
 *     Function to initialize non-finites,
 *     (Inf, NaN and -Inf).
 */

real_T rtInf;
real_T rtMinusInf;
real_T rtNaN;
```

```
real32_T rtInfF;
real32_T rtMinusInfF;
real32_T rtNaNF;

/*
 * Initialize the rtInf, rtMinusInf, and rtNaN needed by the
 * generated code. NaN is initialized as non-signaling. Assumes IEEE.
 */
void rt_InitInfAndNaN(size_t realSize)
{
  (void) (realSize);
  rtNaN = rtGetNaN();
  rtNaNF = rtGetNaNF();
  rtInf = rtGetInf();
  rtInfF = rtGetInfF();
  rtMinusInf = rtGetMinusInf();
  rtMinusInfF = rtGetMinusInfF();
}

/* Test if value is infinite */
boolean_T rtIsInf(real_T value)
{
  return (boolean_T)((value==rtInf || value==rtMinusInf) ? 1U : 0U);
}

/* Test if single-precision value is infinite */
boolean_T rtIsInfF(real32_T value)
{
  return (boolean_T)(((value)==rtInfF || (value)==rtMinusInfF) ? 1U : 0U);
}

/* Test if value is not a number */
boolean_T rtIsNaN(real_T value)
{
  return (boolean_T)((value!=value) ? 1U : 0U);
}

/* Test if single-precision value is not a number */
boolean_T rtIsNaNF(real32_T value)
{
  return (boolean_T)(((value!=value) ? 1U : 0U));
}

/*
 * File trailer for generated code.
 *
 * [EOF]
 */


/*
 * File: rtGetInf.c
 *
 * Code generated for Simulink model 'SVC_Controller'.
 *
```

```
 * Model version              : 1.47
 * Simulink Coder version     : 8.11 (R2016b) 25-Aug-2016
 * C/C++ source code generated on : Tue Jun 25 06:10:03 2024
 *
 * Target selection: ert.tlc
 * Embedded hardware selection: Intel->x86-64 (Windows64)
 * Code generation objectives: Unspecified
 * Validation result: Not run
 */

/*
 * Abstract:
 *      Function to initialize non-finite, Inf
 */

#define NumBitsPerChar          8U

/*
 * Initialize rtInf needed by the generated code.
 * Inf is initialized as non-signaling. Assumes IEEE.
 */
real_T rtGetInf(void)
{
  size_t bitsPerReal = sizeof(real_T) * (NumBitsPerChar);
  real_T inf = 0.0;
  if (bitsPerReal == 32U) {
    inf = rtGetInfF();
  } else {
    union {
      LittleEndianIEEEDouble bitVal;
      real_T fltVal;
    } tmpVal;

    tmpVal.bitVal.words.wordH = 0x7FF00000U;
    tmpVal.bitVal.words.wordL = 0x00000000U;
    inf = tmpVal.fltVal;
  }

  return inf;
}

/*
 * Initialize rtInfF needed by the generated code.
 * Inf is initialized as non-signaling. Assumes IEEE.
 */
real32_T rtGetInfF(void)
{
  IEEESingle infF;
  infF.wordL.wordLuint = 0x7F800000U;
  return infF.wordL.wordLreal;
}

/*
 * Initialize rtMinusInf needed by the generated code.
 * Inf is initialized as non-signaling. Assumes IEEE.
```

```
 */
real_T rtGetMinusInf(void)
{
  size_t bitsPerReal = sizeof(real_T) * (NumBitsPerChar);
  real_T minf = 0.0;
  if (bitsPerReal == 32U) {
    minf = rtGetMinusInfF();
  } else {
    union {
      LittleEndianIEEEDouble bitVal;
      real_T fltVal;
    } tmpVal;

    tmpVal.bitVal.words.wordH = 0xFFF00000U;
    tmpVal.bitVal.words.wordL = 0x00000000U;
    minf = tmpVal.fltVal;
  }

  return minf;
}

/*
 * Initialize rtMinusInfF needed by the generated code.
 * Inf is initialized as non-signaling. Assumes IEEE.
 */
real32_T rtGetMinusInfF(void)
{
  IEEESingle minfF;
  minfF.wordL.wordLuint = 0xFF800000U;
  return minfF.wordL.wordLreal;
}
/*
 * File trailer for generated code.
 *
 * [EOF]
 */


/*
 * File: rtGetNaN.c
 *
 * Code generated for Simulink model 'SVC_Controller'.
 *
 * Model version          : 1.47
 * Simulink Coder version      : 8.11 (R2016b) 25-Aug-2016
 * C/C++ source code generated on : Tue Jun 25 06:10:03 2024
 *
 * Target selection: ert.tlc
 * Embedded hardware selection: Intel->x86-64 (Windows64)
 * Code generation objectives: Unspecified
 * Validation result: Not run
 */

/*
 * Abstract:
```

```
 *      Function to initialize non-finite, NaN
 */

#define NumBitsPerChar          8U

/*
 * Initialize rtNaN needed by the generated code.
 * NaN is initialized as non-signaling. Assumes IEEE.
 */
real_T rtGetNaN(void)
{
  size_t bitsPerReal = sizeof(real_T) * (NumBitsPerChar);
  real_T nan = 0.0;
  if (bitsPerReal == 32U) {
   nan = rtGetNaNF();
  } else {
    union {
      LittleEndianIEEEDouble bitVal;
      real_T fltVal;
    } tmpVal;

    tmpVal.bitVal.words.wordH = 0xFFF80000U;
    tmpVal.bitVal.words.wordL = 0x00000000U;
    nan = tmpVal.fltVal;
  }
  return nan;
}

/*
 * Initialize rtNaNF needed by the generated code.
 * NaN is initialized as non-signaling. Assumes IEEE.
 */
real32_T rtGetNaNF(void)
{
  IEEESingle nanF = { { 0 } };

  nanF.wordL.wordLuint = 0xFFC00000U;
  return nanF.wordL.wordLreal;
}

/*
 * File trailer for generated code.
 *
 * [EOF]
 */


void setup() {
  // put your setup code here, to run once:

  Serial.begin(9600);
  pinMode(Vab,INPUT);
  pinMode(Vbc,INPUT);
  pinMode(Vca,INPUT);
  pinMode(ITCRa,INPUT);
```

```
  pinMode(ITCRb,INPUT);
  pinMode(ITCRc,INPUT);
  pinMode(ISa,INPUT);
  pinMode(ISb,INPUT);
  pinMode(ISc,INPUT);
  pinMode(Ta1,OUTPUT);
  pinMode(Tb1,OUTPUT);
  pinMode(Tc1,OUTPUT);
  pinMode(Ta2,OUTPUT);
  pinMode(Tb2,OUTPUT);
  pinMode(Tc2,OUTPUT);

  SVC_Controller_initialize();

}

void loop() {
  // put your main code here, to run repeatedly:
  VabValue = analogRead(Vab);
  VabValue = (VabValue/1023-2.5)*125;
  SVC_Controller_U.Vab = VabValue;

  VbcValue = analogRead(Vbc);
  VbcValue = (VabValue/1023-2.5)*125;
  SVC_Controller_U.Vbc = VbcValue;

  VcaValue = analogRead(Vca);
  VcaValue = (VcaValue/1023-2.5)*125;
  SVC_Controller_U.Vca = VcaValue;

  ITCRaValue = analogRead(ITCRa);
  ITCRaValue = (ITCRaValue/1023-2.5)*4;
  SVC_Controller_U.ITCRa = ITCRaValue;

  ITCRbValue = analogRead(ITCRb);
  ITCRbValue = (ITCRbValue/1023-2.5)*4;
  SVC_Controller_U.ITCRb = ITCRbValue;

  ITCRcValue = analogRead(ITCRc);
  ITCRcValue = (ITCRcValue/1023-2.5)*4;
  SVC_Controller_U.ITCRc = ITCRcValue;

  ISaValue = analogRead(ISa);
  ISaValue = (ISaValue/1023-2.5)*16;
  SVC_Controller_U.ISa = ISaValue;

  ISbValue = analogRead(ISb);
  ISbValue = (ISbValue/1023-2.5)*16;
  SVC_Controller_U.ISb = ISbValue;

  IScValue = analogRead(ISc);
  IScValue = (IScValue/1023-2.5)*16;
  SVC_Controller_U.ISc = IScValue;

  SVC_Controller_step();
```

```c
  Ta1Val = 255*SVC_Controller_Y.Ta1;
  analogWrite(Ta1,Ta1Val);

  Tb1Val = 255*SVC_Controller_Y.Tb1;
  analogWrite(Tb1,Tb1Val);

  Tc1Val = 255*SVC_Controller_Y.Tc1;
  analogWrite(Tc1,Tc1Val);

  Ta2Val = 255*SVC_Controller_Y.Ta2;
  analogWrite(Ta2,Ta2Val);

  Tb2Val = 255*SVC_Controller_Y.Tb2;
  analogWrite(Tb2,Tb2Val);

  Tc2Val = 255*SVC_Controller_Y.Tc2;
  analogWrite(Tc2,Tc2Val);

  delayMicroseconds(10);

}

/*
 * File: SVC_Controller.c
 *
 * Code generated for Simulink model 'SVC_Controller'.
 *
 * Model version            : 1.47
 * Simulink Coder version    : 8.11 (R2016b) 25-Aug-2016
 * C/C++ source code generated on : Tue Jun 25 06:10:03 2024
 *
 * Target selection: ert.tlc
 * Embedded hardware selection: Intel->x86-64 (Windows64)
 * Code generation objectives: Unspecified
 * Validation result: Not run
 */

/* Block signals (auto storage) */
B_SVC_Controller_T SVC_Controller_B;

/* Block states (auto storage) */
DW_SVC_Controller_T SVC_Controller_DW;

/* External inputs (root inport signals with auto storage) */
ExtU_SVC_Controller_T SVC_Controller_U;

/* External outputs (root outports fed by signals with auto storage) */
ExtY_SVC_Controller_T SVC_Controller_Y;

/* Real-time model */
RT_MODEL_SVC_Controller_T SVC_Controller_M_;
RT_MODEL_SVC_Controller_T *const SVC_Controller_M = &SVC_Controller_M_;
real_T look1_binlxpw(real_T u0, const real_T bp0[], const real_T table[],
             uint32_T maxIndex)
```

```
{
  real_T frac;
  uint32_T iRght;
  uint32_T iLeft;
  uint32_T bpIdx;

  /* Lookup 1-D
     Search method: 'binary'
     Use previous index: 'off'
     Interpolation method: 'Linear'
     Extrapolation method: 'Linear'
     Use last breakpoint for index at or above upper limit: 'off'
     Remove protection against out-of-range input in generated code: 'off'
   */
  /* Prelookup - Index and Fraction
     Index Search method: 'binary'
     Extrapolation method: 'Linear'
     Use previous index: 'off'
     Use last breakpoint for index at or above upper limit: 'off'
     Remove protection against out-of-range input in generated code: 'off'
   */
  if (u0 <= bp0[0U]) {
    iLeft = 0U;
    frac = (u0 - bp0[0U]) / (bp0[1U] - bp0[0U]);
  } else if (u0 < bp0[maxIndex]) {
    /* Binary Search */
    bpIdx = maxIndex >> 1U;
    iLeft = 0U;
    iRght = maxIndex;
    while (iRght - iLeft > 1U) {
      if (u0 < bp0[bpIdx]) {
        iRght = bpIdx;
      } else {
        iLeft = bpIdx;
      }

      bpIdx = (iRght + iLeft) >> 1U;
    }

    frac = (u0 - bp0[iLeft]) / (bp0[iLeft + 1U] - bp0[iLeft]);
  } else {
    iLeft = maxIndex - 1U;
    frac = (u0 - bp0[maxIndex - 1U]) / (bp0[maxIndex] - bp0[maxIndex - 1U]);
  }

  /* Interpolation 1-D
     Interpolation method: 'Linear'
     Use last breakpoint for index at or above upper limit: 'off'
     Overflow mode: 'portable wrapping'
   */
  return (table[iLeft + 1U] - table[iLeft]) * frac + table[iLeft];
}

/*
 * Output and update for enable system:
```

```
*     '<S8>/Subsystem - pi//2 delay'
*     '<S14>/Subsystem - pi//2 delay'
*     '<S20>/Subsystem - pi//2 delay'
*     '<S26>/Subsystem - pi//2 delay'
*/
void SVC_Controlle_Subsystempi2delay(uint8_T rtu_Enable, const real_T
  rtu_alpha_beta[2], real_T rtu_wt, B_Subsystempi2delay_SVC_Contr_T *localB)
{
  /* Outputs for Enabled SubSystem: '<S8>/Subsystem - pi//2 delay' incorporates:
   * EnablePort: '<S12>/Enable'
   */
  if (rtu_Enable > 0) {
    /* Fcn: '<S12>/Fcn' */
    localB->Fcn = rtu_alpha_beta[0] * sin(rtu_wt) - rtu_alpha_beta[1] * cos
      (rtu_wt);

    /* Fcn: '<S12>/Fcn1' */
    localB->Fcn1 = rtu_alpha_beta[0] * cos(rtu_wt) + rtu_alpha_beta[1] * sin
      (rtu_wt);
  }

  /* End of Outputs for SubSystem: '<S8>/Subsystem - pi//2 delay' */
}

/*
 * Output and update for enable system:
 *     '<S8>/Subsystem1'
 *     '<S14>/Subsystem1'
 *     '<S20>/Subsystem1'
 *     '<S26>/Subsystem1'
 */
void SVC_Controller_Subsystem1(uint8_T rtu_Enable, const real_T rtu_
alpha_beta[2],
  real_T rtu_wt, B_Subsystem1_SVC_Controller_T *localB)
{
  /* Outputs for Enabled SubSystem: '<S8>/Subsystem1' incorporates:
   * EnablePort: '<S13>/Enable'
   */
  if (rtu_Enable > 0) {
    /* Fcn: '<S13>/Fcn' */
    localB->Fcn = rtu_alpha_beta[0] * cos(rtu_wt) + rtu_alpha_beta[1] * sin
      (rtu_wt);

    /* Fcn: '<S13>/Fcn1' */
    localB->Fcn1 = -rtu_alpha_beta[0] * sin(rtu_wt) + rtu_alpha_beta[1] * cos
      (rtu_wt);
  }

  /* End of Outputs for SubSystem: '<S8>/Subsystem1' */
}

real_T rt_roundd_snf(real_T u)
{
  real_T y;
  if (fabs(u) < 4.503599627370496E+15) {
```

```
  if (u >= 0.5) {
    y = floor(u + 0.5);
  } else if (u > -0.5) {
    y = u * 0.0;
  } else {
    y = ceil(u - 0.5);
  }
} else {
  y = u;
}

return y;
}

real_T rt_modd_snf(real_T u0, real_T u1)
{
  real_T y;
  real_T tmp;
  if (u1 == 0.0) {
    y = u0;
  } else if (!((!rtIsNaN(u0)) && (!rtIsInf(u0)) && ((!rtIsNaN(u1)) && (!rtIsInf
             (u1))))) {
    y = (rtNaN);
  } else {
    tmp = u0 / u1;
    if (u1 <= floor(u1)) {
      y = u0 - floor(tmp) * u1;
    } else if (fabs(tmp - rt_roundd_snf(tmp)) <= DBL_EPSILON * fabs(tmp)) {
      y = 0.0;
    } else {
      y = (tmp - floor(tmp)) * u1;
    }
  }

  return y;
}

/* Model step function */
void SVC_Controller_step(void)
{
  int_T idxDelay;
  boolean_T rtb_Delay1;
  boolean_T rtb_Delay2;
  real_T rtb_MathFunction;
  real_T rtb_Gain1[3];
  real_T rtb_Sum;
  boolean_T rtb_LogicalOperator;
  real_T rtb_Switch_idx_1;
  real_T rtb_Switch_j_idx_0;
  real_T tmp;

  /* Delay: '<S1>/Delay1' */
  rtb_Delay1 = SVC_Controller_DW.Delay1_DSTATE[0];

  /* Outport: '<Root>/Tc1' incorporates:
```

```
 *  DataTypeConversion: '<S1>/Data Type Conversion'
 *  Delay: '<S1>/Delay1'
 */
SVC_Controller_Y.Tc1 = SVC_Controller_DW.Delay1_DSTATE[0];

/* Delay: '<S1>/Delay2' */
rtb_Delay2 = SVC_Controller_DW.Delay2_DSTATE[0];

/* Outport: '<Root>/Ta1' incorporates:
 *  DataTypeConversion: '<S1>/Data Type Conversion5'
 *  Delay: '<S1>/Delay2'
 */
SVC_Controller_Y.Ta1 = SVC_Controller_DW.Delay2_DSTATE[0];

/* Math: '<S2>/Math Function' incorporates:
 *  Constant: '<S2>/Constant2'
 *  DiscreteIntegrator: '<S2>/Discrete-Time Integrator'
 */
rtb_MathFunction = rt_modd_snf(SVC_Controller_DW.Discrete
TimeIntegrator_DSTATE,
  6.2831853071795862);
for (idxDelay = 0; idxDelay < 3; idxDelay++) {
  /* Gain: '<S27>/Gain1' incorporates:
   *  Gain: '<S27>/Gain3'
   *  Inport: '<Root>/ISa'
   *  Inport: '<Root>/ISb'
   *  Inport: '<Root>/ISc'
   */
  rtb_Gain1[idxDelay] = 0.66666666666666663 *
    (SVC_Controller_ConstP.pooled4[idxDelay + 6] * SVC_Controller_U.ISc
    +
    (SVC_Controller_ConstP.pooled4[idxDelay + 3] * SVC_Controller_U.ISb
    +
    SVC_Controller_ConstP.pooled4[idxDelay] * SVC_Controller_U.ISa));
}

/* Outputs for Enabled SubSystem: '<S26>/Subsystem1' */
SVC_Controller_Subsystem1(SVC_Controller_ConstB.Compare, &rtb_
Gain1[0],
  rtb_MathFunction, &SVC_Controller_B.Subsystem1);

/* End of Outputs for SubSystem: '<S26>/Subsystem1' */

/* Outputs for Enabled SubSystem: '<S26>/Subsystem - pi//2 delay' */
SVC_Controlle_Subsystempi2delay(SVC_Controller_ConstB.Compare_p,
  &rtb_Gain1[0],
  rtb_MathFunction, &SVC_Controller_B.Subsystempi2delay);

/* End of Outputs for SubSystem: '<S26>/Subsystem - pi//2 delay' */

/* Switch: '<S26>/Switch' */
if (SVC_Controller_ConstB.Compare != 0) {
  rtb_Switch_idx_1 = SVC_Controller_B.Subsystem1.Fcn1;
} else {
  rtb_Switch_idx_1 = SVC_Controller_B.Subsystempi2delay.Fcn1;
```

```
}

/* End of Switch: '<S26>/Switch' */
for (idxDelay = 0; idxDelay < 3; idxDelay++) {
  /* Gain: '<S15>/Gain1' incorporates:
   *  Gain: '<S15>/Gain3'
   *  Inport: '<Root>/Vab'
   *  Inport: '<Root>/Vbc'
   *  Inport: '<Root>/Vca'
   */
  rtb_Gain1[idxDelay] = 0.66666666666666663 *
    (SVC_Controller_ConstP.pooled4[idxDelay + 6] * SVC_Controller_
    U.Vca +
    (SVC_Controller_ConstP.pooled4[idxDelay + 3] * SVC_Controller_
    U.Vbc +
    SVC_Controller_ConstP.pooled4[idxDelay] * SVC_Controller_U.Vab));
}

/* Outputs for Enabled SubSystem: '<S14>/Subsystem1' */
SVC_Controller_Subsystem1(SVC_Controller_ConstB.Compare_d, &rtb_
Gain1[0],
  rtb_MathFunction, &SVC_Controller_B.Subsystem1_f);

/* End of Outputs for SubSystem: '<S14>/Subsystem1' */

/* Outputs for Enabled SubSystem: '<S14>/Subsystem - pi//2 delay' */
SVC_Controlle_Subsystempi2delay(SVC_Controller_ConstB.Compare_e,
 &rtb_Gain1[0],
  rtb_MathFunction, &SVC_Controller_B.Subsystempi2delay_b);

/* End of Outputs for SubSystem: '<S14>/Subsystem - pi//2 delay' */

/* Switch: '<S14>/Switch' */
if (SVC_Controller_ConstB.Compare_d != 0) {
  rtb_Switch_j_idx_0 = SVC_Controller_B.Subsystem1_f.Fcn;
} else {
  rtb_Switch_j_idx_0 = SVC_Controller_B.Subsystempi2delay_b.Fcn;
}

/* End of Switch: '<S14>/Switch' */
for (idxDelay = 0; idxDelay < 3; idxDelay++) {
  /* Gain: '<S21>/Gain1' incorporates:
   *  Gain: '<S21>/Gain3'
   *  Inport: '<Root>/ITCRa'
   *  Inport: '<Root>/ITCRb'
   *  Inport: '<Root>/ITCRc'
   */
  rtb_Gain1[idxDelay] = 0.66666666666666663 *
    (SVC_Controller_ConstP.pooled4[idxDelay + 6] * SVC_Controller_
    U.ITCRc +
    (SVC_Controller_ConstP.pooled4[idxDelay + 3] * SVC_Controller_
    U.ITCRb +
    SVC_Controller_ConstP.pooled4[idxDelay] * SVC_Controller_
    U.ITCRa));
}
```

71

```
/* Outputs for Enabled SubSystem: '<S20>/Subsystem1' */
SVC_Controller_Subsystem1(SVC_Controller_ConstB.Compare_j, &rtb_Gain1[0],
  rtb_MathFunction, &SVC_Controller_B.Subsystem1_fj);

/* End of Outputs for SubSystem: '<S20>/Subsystem1' */

/* Outputs for Enabled SubSystem: '<S20>/Subsystem - pi//2 delay' */
SVC_Controlle_Subsystempi2delay(SVC_Controller_ConstB.Compare_g,
 &rtb_
Gain1[0],
  rtb_MathFunction, &SVC_Controller_B.Subsystempi2delay_d);

/* End of Outputs for SubSystem: '<S20>/Subsystem - pi//2 delay' */

/* Sum: '<Root>/Sum' incorporates:
 *  Constant: '<Root>/Constant'
 *  Gain: '<Root>/Gain'
 */
rtb_Sum = -0.03236245954692557 * rtb_Switch_j_idx_0 - 10.0;

/* Switch: '<S20>/Switch' */
if (SVC_Controller_ConstB.Compare_j != 0) {
  tmp = SVC_Controller_B.Subsystem1_fj.Fcn1;
} else {
  tmp = SVC_Controller_B.Subsystempi2delay_d.Fcn1;
}

/* End of Switch: '<S20>/Switch' */

/* Sum: '<Root>/Sum3' incorporates:
 *  DiscreteIntegrator: '<Root>/Discrete-Time Integrator'
 *  Gain: '<Root>/Gain2'
 *  Product: '<Root>/Divide'
 *  Product: '<Root>/Divide1'
 *  Sum: '<Root>/Sum1'
 *  Sum: '<Root>/Sum2'
 */
rtb_Switch_idx_1 = ((0.5 * rtb_Sum +
              SVC_Controller_DW.DiscreteTimeIntegrator_DSTATE_k) + tmp /
             rtb_Switch_j_idx_0) - rtb_Switch_idx_1 /
  rtb_Switch_j_idx_0;

/* Saturate: '<Root>/Saturation' */
if (rtb_Switch_idx_1 > 10.0) {
  rtb_Switch_idx_1 = 10.0;
} else {
  if (rtb_Switch_idx_1 < -10.0) {
    rtb_Switch_idx_1 = -10.0;
  }
}

/* End of Saturate: '<Root>/Saturation' */

/* Gain: '<S1>/Gain' incorporates:
```

```
 *  Lookup_n-D: '<Root>/1-D Lookup Table'
 */
rtb_Switch_idx_1 = 0.017453292519943295 * look1_binlxpw(rtb_Switch
_idx_1,
  SVC_Controller_ConstP.uDLookupTable_bp01Data,
  SVC_Controller_ConstP.uDLookupTable_tableData, 20U);

/* Logic: '<S1>/Logical Operator' incorporates:
 *  Constant: '<S1>/Constant'
 *  RelationalOperator: '<S1>/Relational Operator'
 *  RelationalOperator: '<S1>/Relational Operator1'
 *  Sum: '<S1>/Sum'
 */
rtb_LogicalOperator = ((rtb_MathFunction >= rtb_Switch_idx_1) &&
  (rtb_MathFunction <= rtb_Switch_idx_1 + 1.0471975511965976));

/* Outport: '<Root>/Tb1' incorporates:
 *  DataTypeConversion: '<S1>/Data Type Conversion3'
 */
SVC_Controller_Y.Tb1 = rtb_LogicalOperator;

/* Outport: '<Root>/Tc2' incorporates:
 *  DataTypeConversion: '<S1>/Data Type Conversion1'
 *  Delay: '<S1>/Delay3'
 */
SVC_Controller_Y.Tc2 = SVC_Controller_DW.Delay3_DSTATE[0];

/* Outport: '<Root>/Ta2' incorporates:
 *  DataTypeConversion: '<S1>/Data Type Conversion4'
 *  Delay: '<S1>/Delay4'
 */
SVC_Controller_Y.Ta2 = SVC_Controller_DW.Delay4_DSTATE[0];

/* Outport: '<Root>/Tb2' incorporates:
 *  DataTypeConversion: '<S1>/Data Type Conversion2'
 *  Delay: '<S1>/Delay'
 */
SVC_Controller_Y.Tb2 = SVC_Controller_DW.Delay_DSTATE[0]n;
for (idxDelay = 0; idxDelay < 3; idxDelay++) {
  /* Gain: '<S9>/Gain1' incorporates:
   *  Gain: '<S9>/Gain3'
   *    Inport: '<Root>/Vab'
   *  Inport: '<Root>/Vbc'
   *  Inport: '<Root>/Vca'
   */
  rtb_Gain1[idxDelay] = 0.66666666666666663 *
    (SVC_Controller_ConstP.pooled4[idxDelay + 6] * SVC_Controller_
    U.Vca +
    (SVC_Controller_ConstP.pooled4[idxDelay + 3] * SVC_Controller_
    U.Vbc +
     SVC_Controller_ConstP.pooled4[idxDelay] * SVC_Controller_U.Vab));
}

/* Outputs for Enabled SubSystem: '<S8>/Subsystem1' */
SVC_Controller_Subsystem1(SVC_Controller_ConstB.Compare_j2, &rtb_
```

```
Gain1[0],
  rtb_MathFunction, &SVC_Controller_B.Subsystem1_a);

/* End of Outputs for SubSystem: '<S8>/Subsystem1' */

/* Outputs for Enabled SubSystem: '<S8>/Subsystem - pi//2 delay' */
SVC_Controlle_Subsystempi2delay(SVC_Controller_ConstB.Compare_gg,
&rtb_Gain1[0],
  rtb_MathFunction, &SVC_Controller_B.Subsystempi2delay_n);

/* End of Outputs for SubSystem: '<S8>/Subsystem - pi//2 delay' */

/* Switch: '<S8>/Switch' */
if (SVC_Controller_ConstB.Compare_j2 != 0) {
  tmp = SVC_Controller_B.Subsystem1_a.Fcn1;
} else {
  tmp = SVC_Controller_B.Subsystempi2delay_n.Fcn1;
}

/* End of Switch: '<S8>/Switch' */

/* Update for Delay: '<S1>/Delay1' */
for (idxDelay = 0; idxDelay < 666; idxDelay++) {
  SVC_Controller_DW.Delay1_DSTATE[idxDelay] =
    SVC_Controller_DW.Delay1_DSTATE[idxDelay + 1];
}

SVC_Controller_DW.Delay1_DSTATE[666] = rtb_LogicalOperator;

/* End of Update for Delay: '<S1>/Delay1' */

/* Update for Delay: '<S1>/Delay2' */
for (idxDelay = 0; idxDelay < 1332; idxDelay++) {
  SVC_Controller_DW.Delay2_DSTATE[idxDelay] =
    SVC_Controller_DW.Delay2_DSTATE[idxDelay + 1];
}

SVC_Controller_DW.Delay2_DSTATE[1332] = rtb_LogicalOperator;

/* End of Update for Delay: '<S1>/Delay2' */

/* Update for DiscreteIntegrator: '<S2>/Discrete-Time Integrator'
  incorporates:
 *  Constant: '<S2>/Constant'
 *  Constant: '<S2>/Constant1'
 *  DiscreteIntegrator: '<S6>/Integrator'
 *  Gain: '<S6>/Proportional Gain'
 *  Sum: '<S2>/Sum'
 *  Sum: '<S2>/Sum1'
 *  Sum: '<S6>/Sum'
 */
SVC_Controller_DW.DiscreteTimeIntegrator_DSTATE += (((0.0 - tmp) *
500.0 +
  SVC_Controller_DW.Integrator_DSTATE) + 314.15926535897933) *
  1.0E-5;
```

```
/* Update for DiscreteIntegrator: '<Root>/Discrete-Time Integrator' */
SVC_Controller_DW.DiscreteTimeIntegrator_DSTATE_k += 1.0E-5 *
rtb_Sum;
for (idxDelay = 0; idxDelay < 999; idxDelay++) {
  /* Update for Delay: '<S1>/Delay3' */
  SVC_Controller_DW.Delay3_DSTATE[idxDelay] =
    SVC_Controller_DW.Delay3_DSTATE[idxDelay + 1];

  /* Update for Delay: '<S1>/Delay4' */
  SVC_Controller_DW.Delay4_DSTATE[idxDelay] =
    SVC_Controller_DW.Delay4_DSTATE[idxDelay + 1];

  /* Update for Delay: '<S1>/Delay' */
  SVC_Controller_DW.Delay_DSTATE[idxDelay] =
    SVC_Controller_DW.Delay_DSTATE[idxDelay + 1];
}

/* Update for Delay: '<S1>/Delay3' */
SVC_Controller_DW.Delay3_DSTATE[999] = rtb_Delay1;

/* Update for Delay: '<S1>/Delay4' */
SVC_Controller_DW.Delay4_DSTATE[999] = rtb_Delay2;

/* Update for Delay: '<S1>/Delay' */
SVC_Controller_DW.Delay_DSTATE[999] = rtb_LogicalOperator;

/* Update for DiscreteIntegrator: '<S6>/Integrator' incorporates:
 *  Constant: '<S2>/Constant'
 *  Gain: '<S6>/Integral Gain'
 *  Sum: '<S2>/Sum'
 */
SVC_Controller_DW.Integrator_DSTATE += (0.0 - tmp) * 10.0 * 1.0E-5;
}

/* Model initialize function */
void SVC_Controller_initialize(void)
{
  /* Registration code */

  /* initialize non-finites */
  rt_InitInfAndNaN(sizeof(real_T));

  /* initialize error status */
  rtmSetErrorStatus(SVC_Controller_M, (NULL));

  /* block I/O */
  (void) memset(((void *) &SVC_Controller_B), 0,
        sizeof(B_SVC_Controller_T));

  /* states (dwork) */
  (void) memset((void *)&SVC_Controller_DW, 0,
        sizeof(DW_SVC_Controller_T));

  /* external inputs */
```

```
(void)memset((void *)&SVC_Controller_U, 0, sizeof(ExtU_SVC_
Controller_T));

/* external outputs */
(void) memset((void *)&SVC_Controller_Y, 0,
        sizeof(ExtY_SVC_Controller_T));
}

/* Model terminate function */
void SVC_Controller_terminate(void)
{
  /* (no terminate code required) */
}

/*
 * File trailer for generated code.
 *
 * [EOF]
 */
```

Now, we can compile the program as depicted in Figure 4.14.

Figure 4.14: Compiling the program in Arduino IDE.

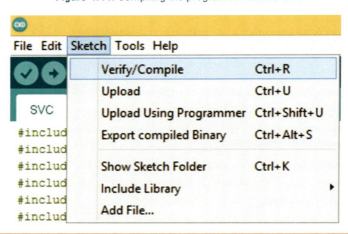

The compiling is done successfully and the hex file is generated to upload inside the Arduino Mega 2560 development board as in Figure 4.15.

Figure 4.15: Successful compiling of the program.

```
Done compiling.
Using library rtGetInf in folder: C:\Users\user\Documents\Arduino\libraries\rtGetInf (legacy)
Using library SVC_Controller_private in folder: C:\Users\user\Documents\Arduino\libraries\SVC_Controller_private (legacy)
Using library rtGetNaN in folder: C:\Users\user\Documents\Arduino\libraries\rtGetNaN (legacy)
"C:\\Program Files (x86)\\Arduino\\hardware\\tools\\avr/bin/avr-size" -A "C:\\Users\\user\\AppData\\Local\\Temp\\arduino_build_14328/SVC.ino.elf"
Sketch uses 9304 bytes (3%) of program storage space. Maximum is 253952 bytes.
Global variables use 5542 bytes (67%) of dynamic memory, leaving 2650 bytes for local variables. Maximum is 8192 bytes.
```

4.4 Continuous-time Code Generation

We can also generate code from the original Simulink schematic illustrated in Figure 2.4 without needing to discretize the three-phase PLL, six-pulse generator and integrator. To do that we insert the control blocks inside a subsystem called SVC_Controller1 as shown in Figure 4.16. The continuous-time code generation files are available in [5].

Figure 4.16: Inserting the control blocks inside a subsystem.

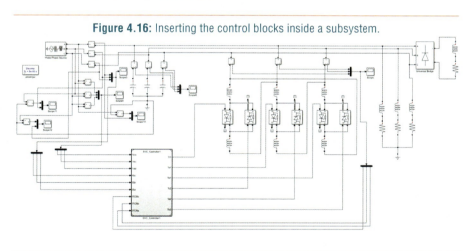

A subsystem SVC_Controller1 schematic is depicted in Figure 4.17.

As you can see in Figure 4.16, we have changed the powergui from continuous to discrete with sampling time, Ts, which is equal to 50 μs. Also, we click on the Model Configuration Parameters icon in the menu and change the solver type from Variable-step to Fixed-step, as illustrated in Figures 3.13 and 3.14, respectively. In the Code Generation section, we click on the Browse... button

Figure 4.17: The subsystem SVC_Controller1 schematic.

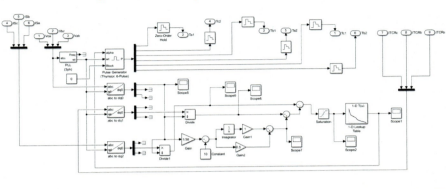

and select Embedded Coder (ert.tlc) as the system target file, then we click on the Apply and OK buttons, respectively, as depicted in Figure 3.15. Also, in the Interface subsection of Code Generation we tick the continuous time option in the Support tab as shown in Figure 4.18.

Figure 4.18: Ticking the continuous time option

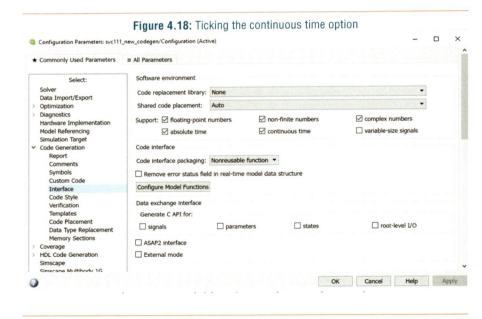

Then, in the All Parameters tab we tick the Support non-inlined S-function option as in Figure 4.19.

Figure 4.19: Ticking the Support non-inlined S-function option.

We also untick the Single output/update function option as depicted in Figure 4.20.

Figure 4.20: Unticking the Single output/update function.

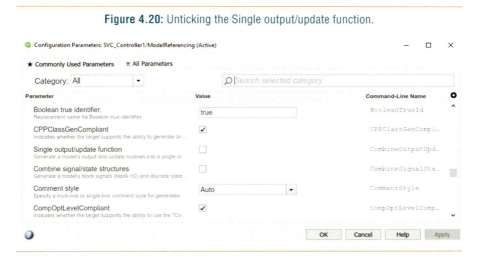

We right click on the subsystem "SVC_Controller1" and select the Block parameters (Subsystem) option as in Figure 3.16. In the pop-up block parameters window we tick on the Treat as atomic unit option, then click on Apply and OK buttons, respectively, as illustrated in Figure 3.17. We right click on the subsystem "SVC_Controller1" and select Subsystem & Model Reference → Convert Subsystem to → Reference Model... options, respectively, as shown in Figure 3.18. In the Model Reference Conversion Advisor window, we click on the Convert button as depicted in Figure 3.19. The conversion of subsystem

"SVC_Controller1" to the reference model is done successfully as you can see in Figure 4.21.

Figure 4.21: The conversion of "SVC_Controller0" to the reference model.

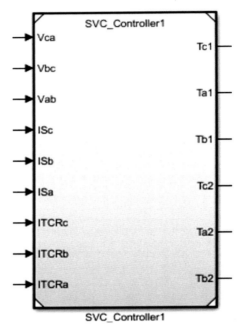

Then inside the subsystem "SVC_Controller1", we can build the model by clicking on the Build Model button as illustrated in Figure 4.22.

The build process is completed successfully as shown in the Diagnostic Viewer window of Figure 4.23.

The Summary and Code Interface Report of Code Generation Report window are depicted in Figures 4.24 and 4.25, respectively.

The generated codes are saved in a folder named "SVC_Controller1_ert_rtw".

Figure 4.22: Clicking on the Build Model button.

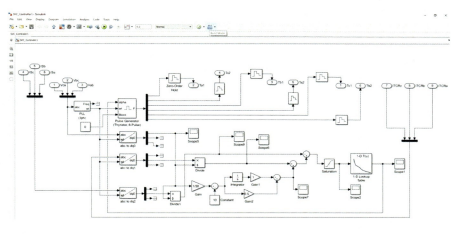

Figure 4.23: Successful build process message in the Diagnostic Viewer window.

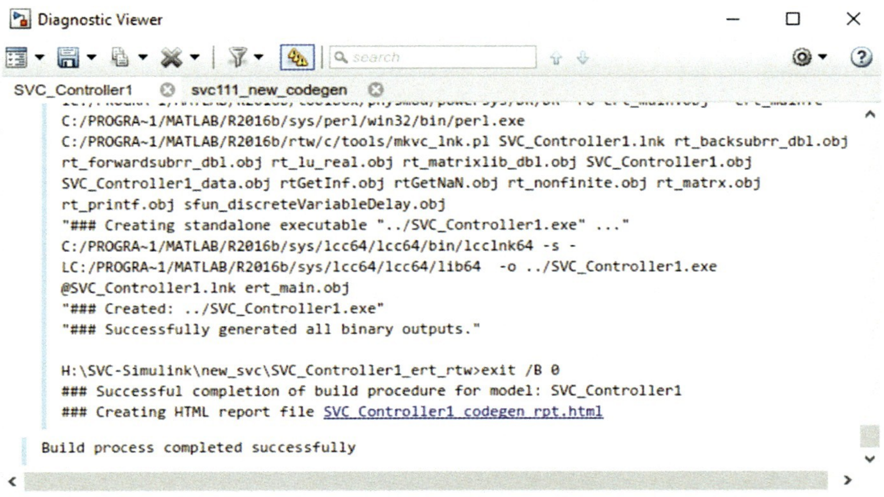

Diagnostic Viewer — □ ✕

SVC_Controller1   svc111_new_codegen

```
C:/PROGRA~1/MATLAB/R2016b/sys/perl/win32/bin/perl.exe
C:/PROGRA~1/MATLAB/R2016b/rtw/c/tools/mkvc_lnk.pl SVC_Controller1.lnk rt_backsubrr_dbl.obj
rt_forwardsubrr_dbl.obj rt_lu_real.obj rt_matrixlib_dbl.obj SVC_Controller1.obj
SVC_Controller1_data.obj rtGetInf.obj rtGetNaN.obj rt_nonfinite.obj rt_matrx.obj
rt_printf.obj sfun_discreteVariableDelay.obj
"### Creating standalone executable "../SVC_Controller1.exe" ..."
C:/PROGRA~1/MATLAB/R2016b/sys/lcc64/lcc64/bin/lcclnk64 -s -
LC:/PROGRA~1/MATLAB/R2016b/sys/lcc64/lcc64/lib64  -o ../SVC_Controller1.exe
@SVC_Controller1.lnk ert_main.obj
"### Created: ../SVC_Controller1.exe"
"### Successfully generated all binary outputs."

H:\SVC-Simulink\new_svc\SVC_Controller1_ert_rtw>exit /B 0
### Successful completion of build procedure for model: SVC_Controller1
### Creating HTML report file SVC_Controller1_codegen_rpt.html
```

Build process completed successfully

Figure 4.24: The Summary of the Code Generation Report window.

Figure 4.25: The Code Interface Report of the Code Generation Report window.

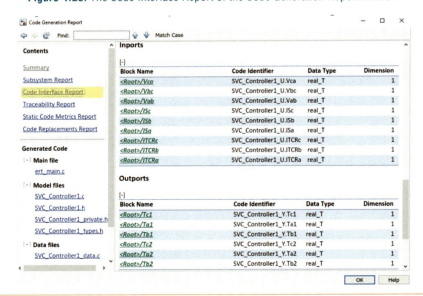

5

DVR Controller Programming in Arduino IDE

5.1 Introduction

Initially, FACTS devices like the static synchronous compensator (STATCOM), static synchronous series compensator (SSSC), interline power flow controller (IPFC), and unified power flow controller (UPFC) were introduced to enhance power quality and system reliability. These devices were originally designed for transmission systems. However, there is now increased focus on improving power quality in distribution systems, leading to the development of custom power devices. Key custom power devices used in distribution systems for power quality enhancement include the distribution static synchronous compensator (DSTATCOM), dynamic voltage restorer (DVR), active power filter (APF), and unified power quality conditioner (UPQC). Power quality in electric networks is a major concern today, with significant economic implications for customers, utilities, and electrical equipment manufacturers. Customers across industrial, commercial, and residential sectors are increasingly affected by power quality issues such as sags, swells, transients, harmonics, and flickers. The rising demand for higher power quality levels is driven by the growing sensitivity of customer needs and expectations. Among modern custom power devices, the dynamic voltage restorer (DVR) is recognized as the most efficient and effective for use in power distribution networks. It offers benefits such as lower costs, smaller size, and rapid dynamic response to disturbances. Numerous studies have addressed the improvement of power quality in power systems using custom power devices. This chapter presents a fuzzy logic-controlled three-phase DVR for improving power quality in three-phase, three-wire systems. The advantage of fuzzy control lies in its reliance on linguistic descriptions rather than requiring a mathematical model of the system. A SIMULINK program has been developed to simulate system operation, and the simulation results demonstrate that the fuzzy controller performs effectively and is highly applicable. The complete set of simulation files and Arduino sketches is available in [5].

5.2 Dynamic Voltage Restorer (DVR)

A DVR, depicted in Figure 5.1, is a custom power device that functions as a harmonic isolator, preventing harmonics in the source voltage from reaching the load. It also balances voltages and provides voltage regulation.

Figure 5.1: Series connected DVR.

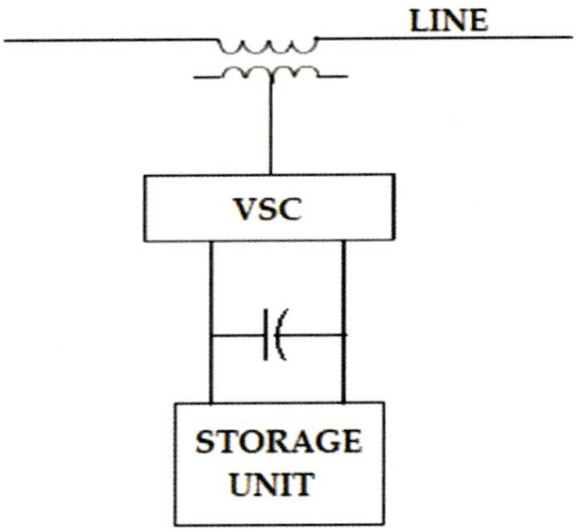

The DVR is a series-connected solid-state device that injects voltage into the system to regulate the load-side voltage. It is installed between the supply and the critical load feeder at the point of common coupling (PCC). Besides compensating for voltage sags and swells, the DVR can also address line voltage harmonics, reduce voltage transients, and suppress fault currents. The DVR's compensation capacity depends on its maximum voltage injection capability and the active power it can supply. When a voltage disturbance occurs, the DVR injects active power or energy into the distribution system. A DC system linked to the inverter input includes a large capacitor for energy storage, which provides reactive power to the load during faults. The equivalent circuit of the DVR is shown in Figure 5.2.

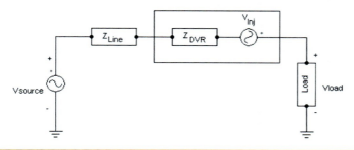

Figure 5.2: Equivalent circuit of the DVR.

From this figure, the injected voltage of the DVR can be expressed as:

$$V_{DVR} = V_{Load} + Z_{Line}.I_{Load} - V_{Source}. \qquad (5.1)$$

The load current is given by

$$I_{Load} = \frac{P_{Load} + jQ_{Load}}{V_{Load}}. \qquad (5.2)$$

The injected voltage of DVR can be written as

$$V_{DVR}\angle a = V_{Load}\angle 0 + I_{Load}.Z_{DVR}\angle(\theta + \beta) - V_{Source}\angle\delta, \qquad (5.3)$$

where α, β, δ and θ are the angles of $V_{DVR}, Z_{DVR}, V_{Source}$ and I_{Load}, respectively, and V_{Load} is considered as a reference voltage. Also, we have

$$\theta = \tan^{-1}\left(\frac{Q_{Load}}{P_{Load}}\right). \qquad (5.4)$$

The complex power injection of DVR can be written as:

$$S_{DVR} = V_{DVR}.I_{Load}^*. \qquad (5.5)$$

5.3 The DVR Control Strategy

The $\alpha - \beta - 0$ transformation is an algebraic transformation of three-phase voltages and currents into a stationary reference frame, also called the Clarke transformation. The $\alpha - \beta - 0$ transformation of a three-phase voltage and its inverse transformation are given by

$$
\begin{bmatrix} v_o \\ v_a \\ v \end{bmatrix} = \sqrt{\frac{2}{3}} \begin{bmatrix} \frac{1}{\sqrt{2}} & \frac{1}{\sqrt{2}} & \frac{1}{\sqrt{2}} \\ 1 & -\frac{1}{2} & -\frac{1}{2} \\ 0 & \frac{\sqrt{3}}{2} & -\frac{\sqrt{3}}{2} \end{bmatrix} \begin{bmatrix} v_a \\ v_b \\ v_c \end{bmatrix}
\tag{5.6}
$$

$$
\begin{bmatrix} v_a \\ v_b \\ v_c \end{bmatrix} = \sqrt{\frac{2}{3}} \begin{bmatrix} \frac{1}{\sqrt{2}} & 1 & 0 \\ \frac{1}{\sqrt{2}} & -\frac{1}{2} & \frac{\sqrt{3}}{2} \\ \frac{1}{\sqrt{2}} & -\frac{1}{2} & -\frac{\sqrt{3}}{2} \end{bmatrix} \begin{bmatrix} v_o \\ v_a \\ v \end{bmatrix}.
\tag{5.7}
$$

Similar equations hold for the line currents i_a, i_b, i_c. One advantage of the $\alpha - \beta - 0$ transformation is the separation of zero sequence components into the 0-axis (v_0 and i_0 variables). The instantaneous powers defined in the $\alpha - \beta - 0$ reference frame is the real power P, the imaginary power q, and the zero-sequence power P_0. They are given by

$$
\begin{bmatrix} P_o \\ P \\ q \end{bmatrix} = \begin{bmatrix} v_o & 0 & 0 \\ 0 & v_a & v \\ 0 & -v & v_a \end{bmatrix} \begin{bmatrix} i_o \\ i_a \\ i \end{bmatrix}.
\tag{5.8}
$$

The instantaneous active three-phase power can be written in terms of $\alpha - \beta - 0$ components as

$$
P_{3f} = v_a.i_a + v_b.i_b + v_c.i_c = v_a.i_a + v.i + v_o.i_o
$$
$$
= P + P_o.
\tag{5.9}
$$

Equation (5.9) shows that the instantaneous active three-phase power $P_{3\phi}$ is always equal to the sum of the real power P and the zero-sequence power P_0. On the other hand, if the $\alpha - \beta$ variables of the imaginary power q defined in (5.8) are replaced by their equivalents in terms of a–b–c variables, the following equation can be written

$$
q = v_\alpha \cdot i_\beta - v_\beta \cdot i_\alpha =
$$
$$
- \frac{1}{\sqrt{3}} \left[(v_a - v_b) \, i_c + (v_b - v_c) \, i_a + (v_c - v_a) \, i_b \right].
\tag{5.10}
$$

A new algorithm to determine the instantaneous reactive currents can be derived from the sub-matrix in (5.8). First, the imaginary power q is calculated directly from (5.10) or from (5.8). Then, the $\alpha-\beta$ reactive currents are calculated as functions of q, v_α and v_β ($P = 0$, $v_0 = 0$ and $P_0 = 0$) as follows.

$$
\begin{bmatrix} i_{qa} \\ i_q \end{bmatrix} = \frac{1}{v_a{}^2 + v^2} \begin{bmatrix} v_a & -v \\ v & v_a \end{bmatrix} \begin{bmatrix} 0 \\ q \end{bmatrix}.
\tag{5.11}
$$

The inverse transformation of $i_{q\alpha}$ and $i_{q\beta}$ results in

$$\begin{bmatrix} i_{qa} \\ i_{qb} \\ i_{qc} \end{bmatrix} = \sqrt{\frac{2}{3}} \begin{bmatrix} 1 & 0 \\ -\frac{1}{2} & \frac{\sqrt{3}}{2} \\ -\frac{1}{2} & -\frac{\sqrt{3}}{2} \end{bmatrix} \begin{bmatrix} i_{qa} \\ i_q \end{bmatrix}. \tag{5.12}$$

Therefore, the three phase voltages that should be injected using DVR are calculated as follows:

$$\begin{bmatrix} v_{ca} \\ v_{cb} \\ v_{cc} \end{bmatrix} = -k \begin{bmatrix} i_{qa} \\ i_{qb} \\ i_{qc} \end{bmatrix}. \tag{5.13}$$

The Fuzzy Logic tool is a mathematical method for managing uncertainty. The fuzzy logic controller (FLC) is well-suited for systems that are inherently challenging to model due to naturally occurring nonlinear behaviors. It utilizes a database composed of membership functions where membership values range between zero (0) and one (1). The key operations include fuzzification, inference mechanism, and defuzzification. The inference mechanism employs a set of linguistic rules to transform input conditions into a fuzzified output. Finally, defuzzification converts these fuzzy outputs into precise, required signals. Fuzzification, a critical concept in fuzzy logic theory, involves converting crisp values into fuzzy values by identifying and addressing uncertainties present in the crisp quantities. The membership functions represent this conversion. Conversely, defuzzification converts fuzzy values back into crisp quantities necessary for further processing since fuzzy results alone are insufficient for many applications. Designing a fuzzy logic controller involves several steps:

1. Identifying the input signals to the FLC.
2. Determining the number of membership functions.
3. Deciding on the type of membership functions.

The number of membership functions affects the quality of control achieved with the FLC; more membership functions enhance control quality but require increased computational time and memory. Studies often consider seven membership functions for each input and output signal. In the fuzzy logic control algorithm for DVR, as shown in Table 5.1, two inputs are necessary: the reference currents (as per equation (5.13)) and the measured output currents of the DVR. These inputs are associated with membership functions, forming forty-nine rules utilized based on the operation. The membership functions are typically labeled as negative large (NL), negative middle (NM), negative small (NS), zero (ZE), positive small (PS), positive middle (PM), and positive large (PL). However, in this paper, the specific membership functions used are detailed as below.

$$\begin{cases} \mu_{in1} = \{NM, ZE, PM\} \\ \mu_{in2} = \{NM, ZE, PM\} \\ \mu_{out1} = \{NM, ZE, PM\} \end{cases} . \tag{5.14}$$

The actual current is compared to the reference current, and any error is corrected by the fuzzy controller. Fuzzy sets provide a flexible approach to membership functions. A triangular membership function, known for its simplicity and ease of implementation, is used in this application. Fuzzy inference involves creating a mapping from a given input to an output using fuzzy logic. The centroid method of defuzzification is also employed in this process.

Table 5.1: The fuzzy rule base.

In2 \ In1	NM	ZE	PM
NM	NM	NM	ZE
ZE	NM	ZE	PM
PM	ZE	PM	PM

5.4 The Simulink Simulation Results

The simulation model of the proposed DVR with $\alpha - \beta - 0$ transformation and fuzzy logic control using MATLAB/Simulink software is shown in Figure 5.3.

The block diagrams of $\alpha - \beta - 0$ transformation to produce DVR reference currents from load voltages and currents are shown in Figures 5.4, 5.5, 5.6, 5.7 and 5.8 respectively.

The block diagram of fuzzy logic control that is applied for creating gate pulse signals of the voltage source inverter using calculated reference currents and the measured output current of the DVR is depicted in Figure 5.9.

The three-phase source block parameters are illustrated in Figure 5.10.

The inductance matrix type three-phase transformer (three-windings) block parameters with star connection (Y) for winding 1 and delta connection (D1) for windings 2 and 3 are shown in Figure 5.11.

Figure 5.3: Proposed DVR with $\alpha - \beta - 0$ transformation and fuzzy logic control.

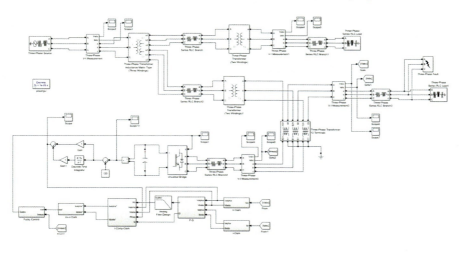

The three-phase transformer (two-windings) block parameters with delta connection (D1) for winding 1 and star connection grounded (Yg) for winding 2 are depicted in Figure 5.12.

Figure 5.4: Load voltages Clarke transformation.

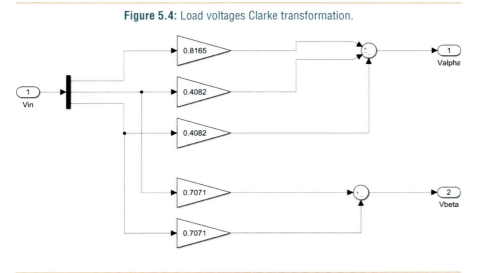

Figure 5.5: Load currents Clarke transformation.

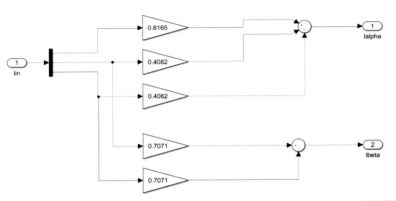

Figure 5.6: Active and reactive power calculation from Clarke transformation.

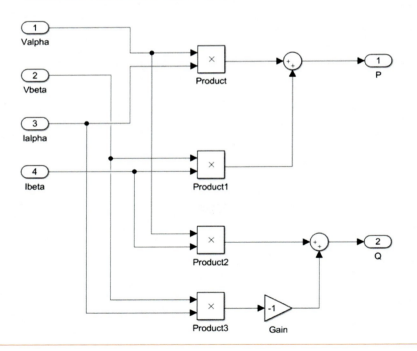

Figure 5.7: Clarke transformation compensated currents.

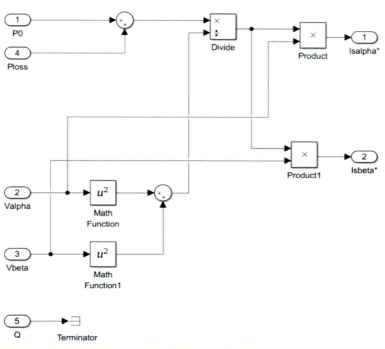

Figure 5.8: Inverse Clarke transformation compensated currents.

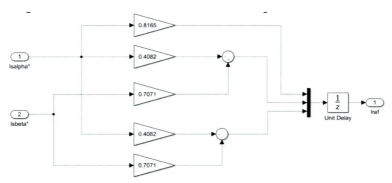

Figure 5.9: Block diagram of creating gate signals using fuzzy logic control.

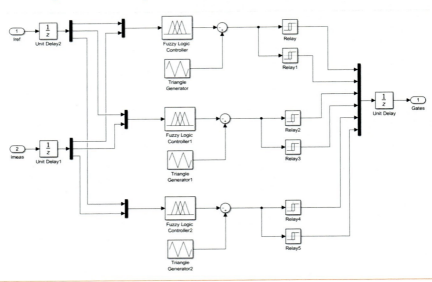

Figure 5.10: The three-phase source block parameters.

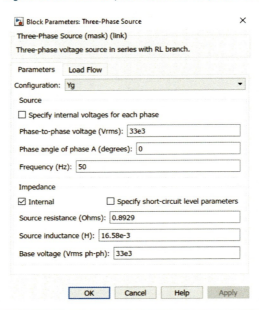

Figure 5.11: Inductance matrix type three-phase transformer block parameters.

Block Parameters: Three-Phase Transformer Inductance Matrix Type (Three Windings)   ×

Three-Phase Transformer Inductance MatrixType (Three Windings) (mask) (link)

This three-phase transformer model represents coupling between windings located on different phases of a three-limb or a five-limb core. It also allows modeling of a three-phase transformer built with three single-phase units (no coupling between phases). The transformer R L parameters are obtained from no-load excitation tests and short-circuit tests in positive- and zero-sequence. When "Three-limb or five-limb" core type is specified, the transformer is modeled by 9 coupled windings; otherwise, it is modeled by 3 sets of 3 coupled windings (Z0=Z1).

Configuration   Parameters

Nominal power and frequency [Pnom(VA), Fnom(Hz)] [35e6, 50]

Nominal line-line voltages [V1, V2, V3] (Vrms) [33e3, 6.6e3, 6.6e3]

Winding resistances [R1, R2, R3] (pu) [0.005, 0.005, 0.005]

Positive-sequence no-load excitation current (% of Inom) 0.06

Positive-sequence no-load losses (W) 35e6*0.04/100

Positive-sequence short-circuit reactances [X12, X13, X23] (pu) [0.087, 0.166, 0.067]

Zero-sequence no-load excitation current with Delta windings opened (% of Inom) 100

Zero-sequence no-load losses with Delta windings opened (W) 35e6*1/100

Zero-sequence short-circuit reactances [X12, X13, X23] (pu) [0.1, 0.2, 0.3]

☐ Zero-sequence X12 measured with winding 3 Delta connected

OK   Cancel   Help   Apply

Figure 5.12: The three-phase transformer (two-windings) block parameters.

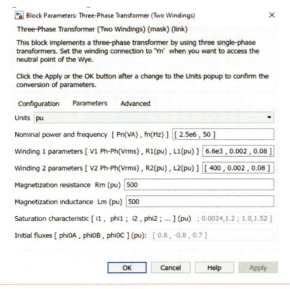

Block Parameters: Three-Phase Transformer (Two Windings)   ×

Three-Phase Transformer (Two Windings) (mask) (link)

This block implements a three-phase transformer by using three single-phase transformers. Set the winding connection to 'Yn' when you want to access the neutral point of the Wye.

Click the Apply or the OK button after a change to the Units popup to confirm the conversion of parameters.

Configuration   Parameters   Advanced

Units pu   ▼

Nominal power and frequency [Pn(VA) , fn(Hz)] [2.5e6 , 50]

Winding 1 parameters [V1 Ph-Ph(Vrms) , R1(pu) , L1(pu)] 6.6e3 , 0.002 , 0.08]

Winding 2 parameters [V2 Ph-Ph(Vrms) , R2(pu) , L2(pu)] [400 , 0.002 , 0.08]

Magnetization resistance Rm (pu) 500

Magnetization inductance Lm (pu) 500

Saturation characteristic [i1 ; phi1 ; i2 , phi2 ; ...] (pu)   ; 0.0024,1.2 ; 1.0,1.52]

Initial fluxes [phi0A , phi0B , phi0C] (pu): [0.8 , -0.8 , 0.7]

OK   Cancel   Help   Apply

The three-phase transformer (12 terminals) block parameters are illustrated in Figure 5.13.

Figure 5.13: The three-phase transformer (12 terminals) block parameters.

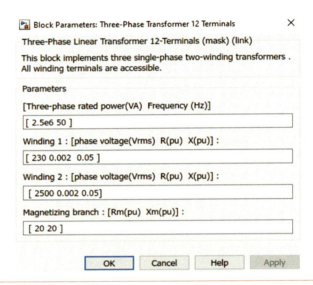

All the three-phase series RL branches have the following parameters:

$$R = 1\ \Omega,\ L = 1\ \text{mH}. \tag{5.15}$$

Also, the DC link capacitor value for the universal IGBT bridge is

$$C = 1\ \text{mF}. \tag{5.16}$$

The analog filter design block parameters are shown in Figure 5.14.

The three-phase series RLC load parameters are depicted in Figure 5.15.

The triangle generator block parameters inside the Fuzzy Control subsystem are illustrated in Figure 5.16.

Also, two relay blocks of each phase in Figure 5.9 complement each other, i.e. for a high gate driving relay, the output when on is 1; however, for a low gate driving relay, the output when on is 0 and vice versa. To design a fuzzy logic

Figure 5.14: The analog filter design block parameters.

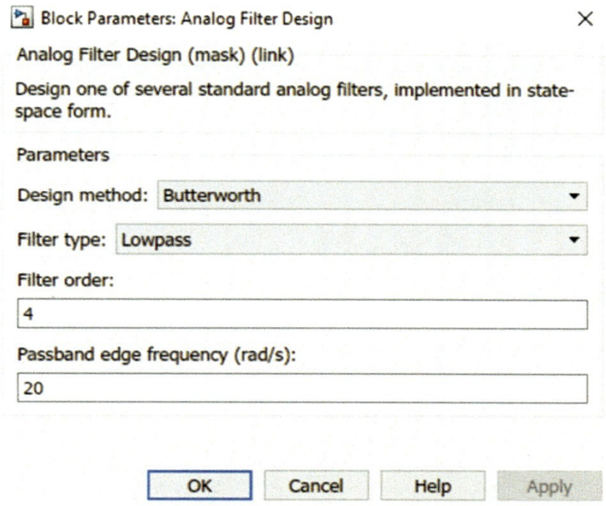

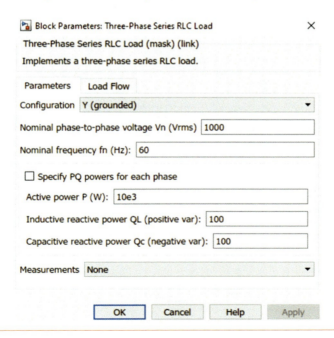

Figure 5.15: The three-phase series RLC load parameters.

Figure 5.16: The triangle generator block parameters.

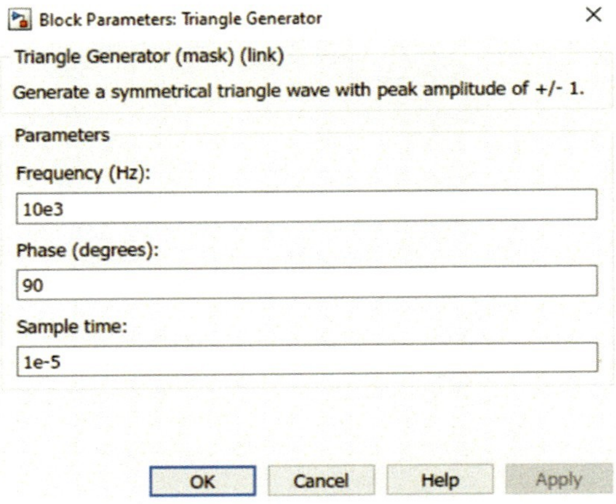

Block Parameters: Triangle Generator   ✕

Triangle Generator (mask) (link)

Generate a symmetrical triangle wave with peak amplitude of +/- 1.

Parameters

Frequency (Hz):

10e3

Phase (degrees):

90

Sample time:

1e-5

| OK | Cancel | Help | Apply |

controller, we enter "fuzzy" in the MATLAB command window. The FIS editor, rule editor, rule viewer and triangular membership function editor are shown in Figures 5.17, 5.18, 5.19, and 5.20, respectively.

Figure 5.17: The FIS editor.

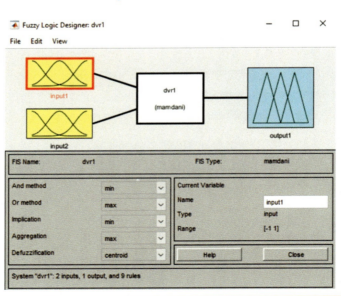

Figure 5.18: The rule editor.

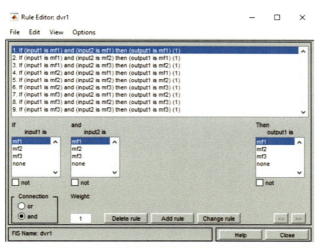

Figure 5.19: The rule viewer.

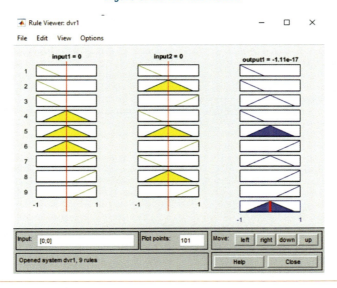

Figure 5.20: The membership function editor.

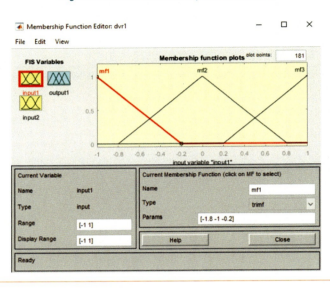

Then we export the designed fuzzy inference system to a file titled "dvr1.fis", as you can see in Figure 5.21.

Figure 5.21: Exporting the designed fuzzy logic controller to a file.

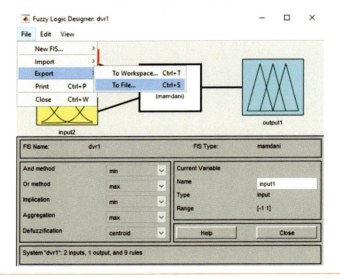

Finally, we specify the saved file directory in the fuzzy logic controller block parameters as depicted in Figure 5.22.

Figure 5.22: Specifying the saved file directory in the fuzzy logic controller.

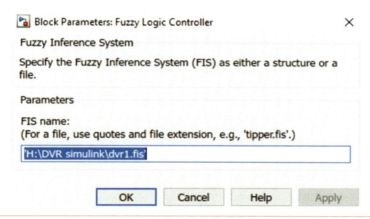

In the simulation study, the following three-phase system as illustrated in Figure 5.23 is considered.

Figure 5.23: Simulation model with a three-phase fault across a load.

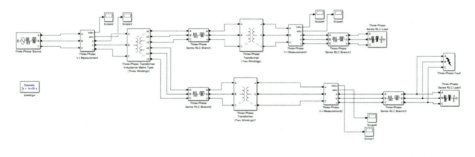

It is assumed that the three-phase fault is applied across a load over 11 to 12 seconds, as depicted in Figure 5.24.

The source voltage and current waveforms are shown in Figures 5.25 and 5.26, respectively.

Now, the proposed DVR is connected to the system as shown in Figure 5.3 and again the three-phase fault is applied across the load during 11 to 12

Figure 5.24: The three-phase fault block parameters.

Block Parameters: Three-Phase Fault   ✕

Three-Phase Fault (mask) (link)

Implements a fault (short-circuit) between any phase and the ground. When the external switching time mode is selected, a Simulink logical signal is used to control the fault operation.

Parameters

Initial status: | 0 |

Fault between:

☑ Phase A   ☑ Phase B   ☑ Phase C   ☑ Ground

Switching times (s): | [11 12] | ☐ External

Fault resistance Ron (Ohm): | 0.001 |

Ground resistance Rg (Ohm): | 0.01 |

Snubber resistance Rs (Ohm): | 1e6 |

Snubber capacitance Cs (F): | inf |

Measurements | None   ▼ |

| OK | Cancel | Help | Apply |

Figure 5.25: Source voltages during 11 s to 12 s of the three-phase fault without DVR.

Figure 5.26: Source currents during 11 s to 12 s of the three-phase fault without DVR.

seconds of simulation time. In this case, the source voltages and currents are depicted in Figures 5.27 and 5.28, respectively.

Figure 5.27: Source voltages during 11 s to 12 s of the three-phase fault with DVR.

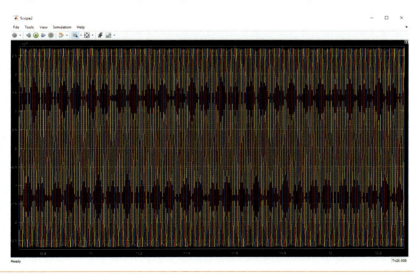

Figure 5.28: Source currents during 11 s to 12 s of the three-phase fault with DVR.

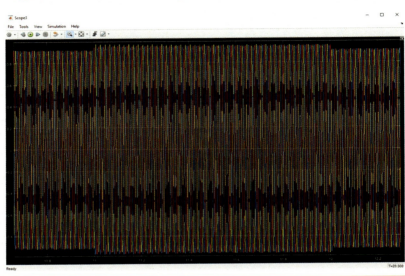

As shown in Figure 5.28, the proposed DVR reduces the source fault currents during the three-phase fault across the load effectively. The proposed

Figure 5.29: The DVR voltages during 11 s to 12 s of the three-phase fault.

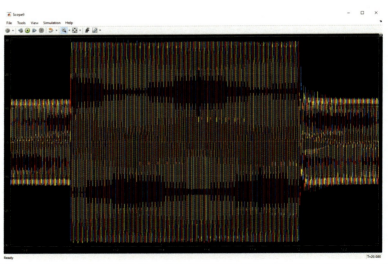

DVR output voltages and currents and also the DC capacitor voltage of DVR during a three-phase fault from 11 to 12 seconds of simulation time are given in Figures 5.29, 5.30 and 5.31, respectively.

Figure 5.30: The DVR currents during 11 s to 12 s of the three-phase fault.

Figure 5.31: The DVR capacitor voltage during 11 s to 12 s of the three-phase fault.

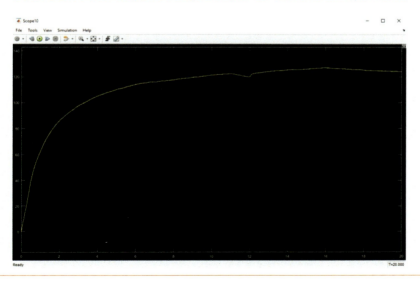

5.5 Code Generation and Arduino Programming

In order to carry out code generation, we put the DVR controller inside a subsystem. Therefore, using a multiplexer and demultiplexer we arrange the control signals as in Figure 5.32.

Figure 5.32: Rearranging the control signals using a multiplexer and demultiplexer.

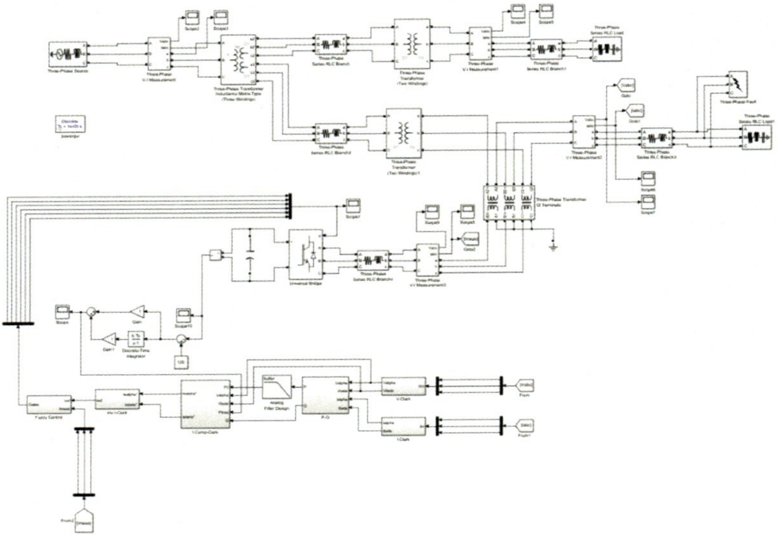

Then we select the DVR controller blocks, and right click and choose the "Create Subsystem from Selection" option as illustrated in Figure 5.33.

The created DVR controller subsystem (DVR_Controller) is shown in Figure 5.34.

The subsystem "DVR_Controller" blocks are depicted in Figure 5.35.

We right click on the subsystem "DVR_Controller" and select the Block parameters (Subsystem) option, as seen in Figure 3.16. In the pop-up block parameters window we tick the Treat as atomic unit option, then click on the Apply and OK buttons, respectively, as illustrated in Figure 3.17. We right click on the subsystem "DVR_Controller" and select Subsystem & Model Reference → Convert Subsystem to → Reference Model… options, respectively, as shown in Figure 3.18. In the Model Reference Conversion Advisor window, we click

Figure 5.33: Creating a subsystem from selected blocks.

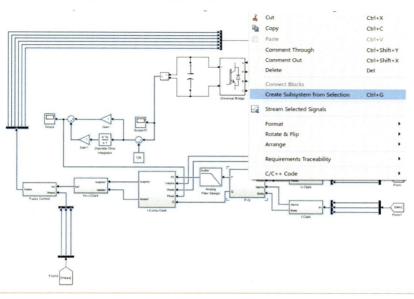

Figure 5.34: The created DVR controller subsystem (DVR_Controller).

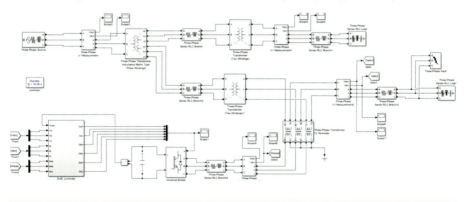

on the Convert button. The conversion of subsystem "DVR_Controller" to the reference model is done successfully, as you can see in Figure 5.36.

The powergui is discrete with sampling time, Ts, which is equal to 10 μs. Also, we click on the Model Configuration Parameters icon in the menu and change the solver type from Variable-step to Fixed-step. In the Code Generation

Figure 5.35: The subsystem "DVR_Controller" blocks.

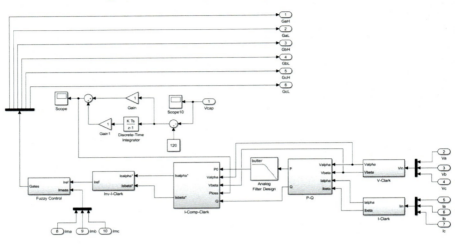

Figure 5.36: The conversion of subsystem "DVR_Controller" to the reference model.

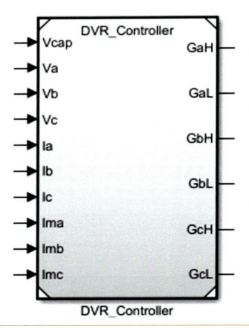

section, we click on the Browse... button and select Embedded Coder (ert.tlc) as the system target file, then we click on the Apply and OK buttons, respectively, as depicted in Figure 3.15. Also, in the Interface subsection of Code Generation we tick the continuous time option in the Support tab, as shown in Figure 4.18.

Then inside the subsystem "DVR_Controller", we build the model by clicking on the Build Model button, as illustrated in Figure 5.37.

Figure 5.37: Clicking on the Build Model button.

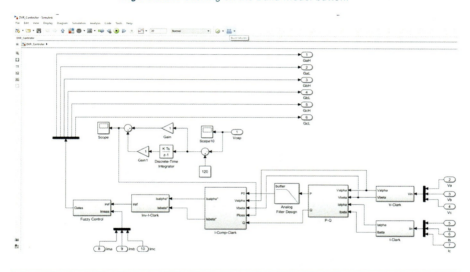

The build process is completed successfully, as shown in the Diagnostic Viewer window of Figure 5.38.

The Summary and Code Interface Report of the Code Generation Report window are depicted in Figures 5.39 and 5.40, respectively.

The generated codes of the previous chapter are saved in a folder named "DVR_Controller_ert_rtw". We copy and paste it into the directory shown in Figure 5.41. This PC → Documents → Arduino.

Then, we create the folders DVR_Controller, DVR_Controller_private and DVR_Controller_types inside the libraries folder. The other folders, i.e. rtwtypes, rtw_solver, rtw_continuous, rt_nonfinite, rtGetInf, and rtGetNaN remain the same as before, as depicted in Figure 5.42.

Figure 5.38: Successful build process message in the Diagnostic Viewer window.

Figure 5.39: The Summary of Code Generation Report window.

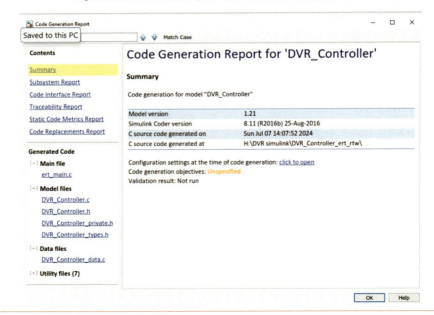

Figure 5.40: The Code Interface Report of the Code Generation Report window.

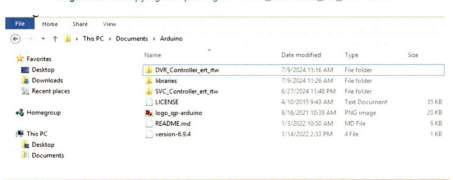

Figure 5.41: Copying and pasting the "DVR_Controller_ert_rtw" folder.

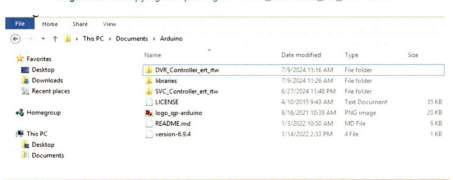

Figure 5.42: Creating some folders inside the libraries folder.

We copy and paste the header files (DVR_Controller.h, DVR_Controller_private.h, and DVR_Controller_types.h) inside the DVR_Controller_ert_rtw folder to the corresponding folders created in Figure 5.42. In this section, we will use the Arduino Mega 2560 development board to program our DVR controller, as you can see in Figure 4.13. We will use the following code structure in Arduino IDE.

```
#include "DVR_Controller.h"
#include "DVR_Controller_private.h"
#include "DVR_Controller.h"
#include "Arduino.h"
#include <stddef.h>
#include <stdio.h>
#include "rtwtypes.h"
#include "rt_nonfinite.h"
#include "rtGetNaN.h"
#include "rtGetInf.h"
int Va = A0;
double VaValue = 0;
int Vb = A1;
double VbValue = 0;

int Vc = A2;
double VcValue = 0;

int Ia = A3;
double IaValue = 0;

int Ib = A4;
double IbValue = 0;

int Ic = A5;
double IcValue = 0;

int Ima = A6;
double ImaValue = 0;

int Imb = A7;
double ImbValue = 0;

int Imc = A8;
double ImcValue = 0;

int Vcap = A9;
double VcapValue = 0;

int GaH = 4;
double GaHVal = 0;

int GaL = 5;
double GaLVal = 0;

int GbH = 6;
```

```
double GbHVal = 0;

int GbL = 7;
double GbLVal = 0;

int GcH = 8;
double GcHVal = 0;

int GcL = 9;
double GcLVal = 0;

/*
 * File: DVR_Controller_data.c
 */

/*
 * File: rt_nonfinite.c
 */

/*
 * File: rtGetInf.c
 */

/*
 * File: rtGetNaN.c
 */


void setup() {
  // put your setup code here, to run once:

  Serial.begin(9600);
  pinMode(Va,INPUT);
  pinMode(Vb,INPUT);
  pinMode(Vc,INPUT);
  pinMode(Ia,INPUT);
  pinMode(Ib,INPUT);
  pinMode(Ic,INPUT);
  pinMode(Ima,INPUT);
  pinMode(Imb,INPUT);
  pinMode(Imc,INPUT);
  pinMode(Vcap,INPUT);
  pinMode(GaH,OUTPUT);
  pinMode(GaL,OUTPUT);
  pinMode(GbH,OUTPUT);
  pinMode(GbL,OUTPUT);
  pinMode(GcH,OUTPUT);
  pinMode(GcL,OUTPUT);

  DVR_Controller_initialize();

}

void loop() {
  // put your main code here, to run repeatedly:
```

```
VaValue = analogRead(Va);
VaValue = (VaValue/1023-2.5)*125;
DVR_Controller_U.Va = VaValue;

VbValue = analogRead(Vb);
VbValue = (VaValue/1023-2.5)*125;
DVR_Controller_U.Vb = VbValue;

VcValue = analogRead(Vc);
VcValue = (VcValue/1023-2.5)*125;
DVR_Controller_U.Vc = VcValue;
IaValue = analogRead(Ia);
IaValue = (IaValue/1023-2.5)*4;
DVR_Controller_U.Ia = IaValue;

IbValue = analogRead(Ib);
IbValue = (IbValue/1023-2.5)*4;
DVR_Controller_U.Ib = IbValue;

IcValue = analogRead(Ic);
IcValue = (IcValue/1023-2.5)*4;
DVR_Controller_U.Ic = IcValue;

ImaValue = analogRead(Ima);
ImaValue = (ImaValue/1023-2.5)*16;
DVR_Controller_U.Ima = ImaValue;

ImbValue = analogRead(Imb);
ImbValue = (ImbValue/1023-2.5)*16;
DVR_Controller_U.Imb = ImbValue;

ImcValue = analogRead(Imc);
ImcValue = (ImcValue/1023-2.5)*16;
DVR_Controller_U.Imc = ImcValue;

VcapValue = analogRead(Vcap);
VcapValue = (VcapValue/1023)*30;
DVR_Controller_U.Vcap = VcapValue;

DVR_Controller_step();

GaHVal = 255*DVR_Controller_Y.GaH;
analogWrite(GaH,GaHVal);

GaLVal = 255*DVR_Controller_Y.GaL;
analogWrite(GaL,GaLVal);

GbHVal = 255*DVR_Controller_Y.GbH;
analogWrite(GbH,GbHVal);

GbLVal = 255*DVR_Controller_Y.GbL;
analogWrite(GbL,GbLVal);

GcHVal = 255*DVR_Controller_Y.GcH;
analogWrite(GcH,GcHVal);
```

```
GcLVal = 255*DVR_Controller_Y.GcL;
analogWrite(GcL,GcLVal);

delayMicroseconds(10);
}

/*
 * File: DVR_Controller.c
 */
```

As highlighted in the code, we should put the codes inside DVR_Controller.c file after the loop function; however, the codes are inside DVR_Controller_data.c, rt_nonfinite.c, rtGetInf, and rtGetNaN files before the setup function. Now, we can compile the program, so the compiling is done successfully and the hex file is generated to upload to the Arduino Mega 2560 development board, as you can see in Figure 5.43.

Figure 5.43: Successful compilation of the program.

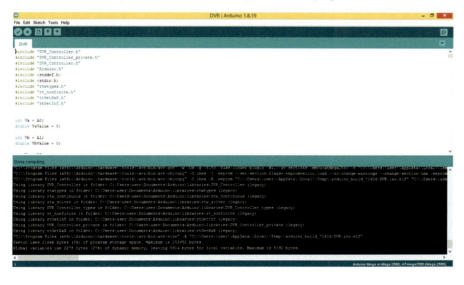

Bibliography

[1]   Z. Shicheng, F. Sian and Z. Gaoyu, "Research on TCR type SVC system and MATLAB simulation," 2010, 5th IEEE Conference on Industrial Electronics and Applications, pp. 2110-2114.

[2]   C. Liu, A. Edris, M. Eremia, Advanced Solutions in Power Systems, 2016.

[3]   https://electronics.stackexchange.com/questions/685811/series-thyristor-circuit

[4]   B. Ram, D. N. Vishwakarma, Power System Protection and Switchgear, McGraw-Hill Publishing Co., 12th reprint, 2004.

[5]   https://github.com/Majid-Pakdel/book-codes

Index

Printed in the United States
by Baker & Taylor Publisher Services